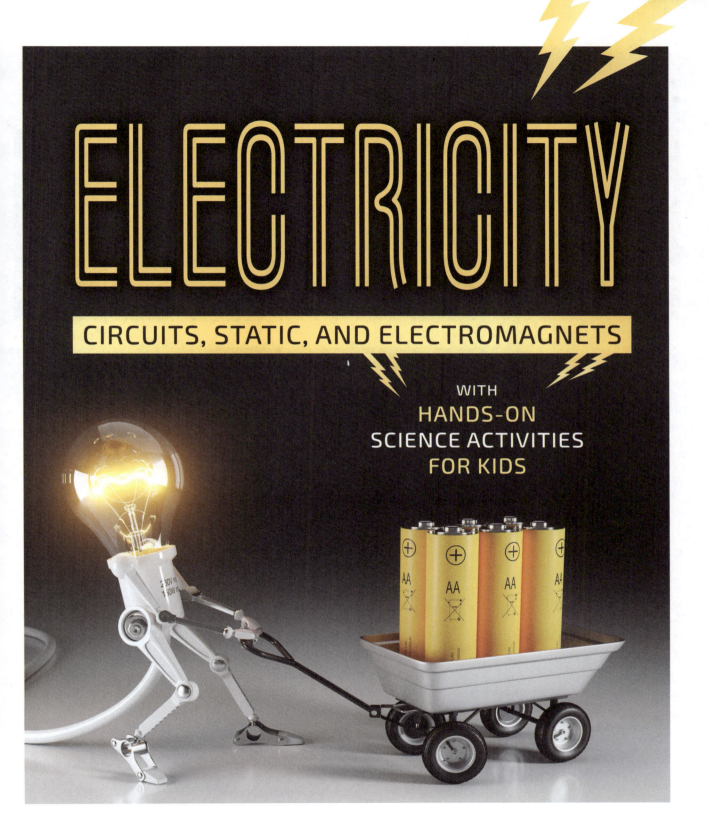

More science titles from Nomad Press

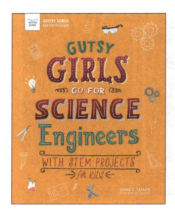 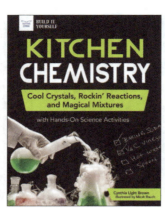 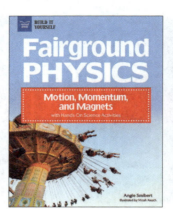 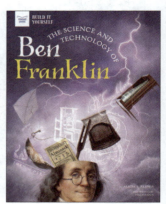

Check out more titles at www.nomadpress.net

Nomad Press

A division of Nomad Communications

10 9 8 7 6 5 4 3 2 1

Copyright © 2022 by Nomad Press. All rights reserved.

No part of this book may be reproduced in any form without permission in writing from the publisher, except by a reviewer who may quote brief passages in a review or **for limited educational use**. The trademark "Nomad Press" and the Nomad Press logo are trademarks of Nomad Communications, Inc.

This book was manufactured by Versa Press, East Peoria, Illinois
October 2022, Job #J22-02803
ISBN Softcover: 978-1-64741-006-3
ISBN Hardcover: 978-1-64741-003-2

Educational Consultant, Marla Conn

Questions regarding the ordering of this book should be addressed to
Nomad Press
PO Box 1036, Norwich, VT 05055
www.nomadpress.net

Printed in the United States.

CONTENTS

Timeline . . . iv

Introduction
The Power of Zap! . . . 1

Chapter 1
Static Electricity . . . 9

Chapter 2
Currents . . . 25

Chapter 3
Circuits . . . 39

Chapter 4
Electromagnetism . . . 55

Chapter 5
Motors and Generators . . . 67

Chapter 6
Earth-Friendly Electricity . . . 81

- **Glossary**
- **Metric Conversions**
- **Resources**
- **Essential Questions**
- **Index**

Interested in primary sources? Look for this icon. PS

Use a smartphone or tablet app to scan the QR code and explore more! Photos can also be primary sources because a photograph takes a picture at the moment something happens. You can find a list of URLs on the Resources page. If the QR code doesn't work, try searching the internet with the Keyword Prompts to find other helpful sources.

🔎 electricity

TIMELINE

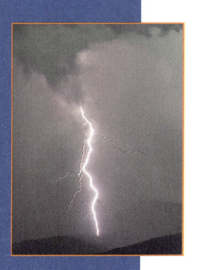

600s BCE: Thales of Miletus recognizes that rubbing wool or fur on amber causes static electricity.

1600s: William Gilbert invents the versorium, an instrument that can detect electrical charges.

1745: German inventor Ewald von Kleist and Pieter van Musschenbroek of Holland separately discover a device that can store an electric charge. This becomes known as the Leyden jar.

1750: Benjamin Franklin begins experimenting with electricity. He later flies a kite in a storm to prove that lightning is an electric charge.

1780: Luigi Galvani demonstrates that an animal's nerves have an electric basis.

1800: Alessandro Volta invents the first chemical battery.

1830: Hans Christian Oersted and Michael Faraday discover the principles of electromagnetism. James Maxwell later combines these principles into a single theory.

1837: The first electric motors are built.

1860: French investor Augustin Mouchot uses mirrors to invent the first solar energy system.

1879: Thomas Edison invents a filament that makes light bulbs an option for households.

1880: Edison Electric Light Company is founded.

1883: James Wimshurst invents a machine that builds up an electric charge.

1895: Nikola Tesla invents a system that alternates electric current.

TIMELINE

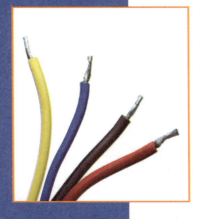

1895: Niagara Falls in New York becomes the first large-scale hydropowered electric plant.

1900–1940: Electric motors are used in appliances such as vacuum cleaners, washing machines, televisions, electric freezers, and air conditioners.

1922: Edith Clarke becomes the first woman professionally employed as an electrical engineer in the United States.

1927: A group of rural U.S. farmers purchases the first commercial wind turbines.

1940s: Electronic computers are invented and the first televisions go on sale.

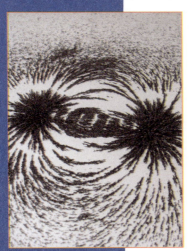

1950s: Grace Murray Hopper is instrumental in the development of COBOL, one of the first computer languages. She had earlier coined the terms "computer bug" and "debugging" to describe fixing a computer problem.

1951: The first nuclear reactor is built and used to generate energy.

1960s: Transistors make portable radios possible.

1990s: Compact fluorescent bulbs grow in popularity, as do wind, solar, hydro, and nuclear power.

2000s: Laptop computers, cell phones, and tablets are all common household items. Smaller batteries that deliver more energy make this technology possible.

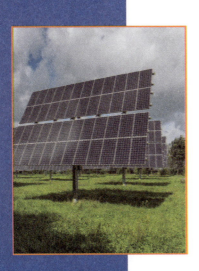

2020s: Researchers develop super tiny robots called nanobots that may be used in science and medicine.

2021: Electric car sales in the United States more than double to 6.6 million, which is almost 9 percent of the global car market.

v

Introduction

THE POWER OF
ZAP!

What is the first thing you did when you woke up this morning? You probably turned on a light or went to the kitchen for breakfast. Maybe someone made you pancakes on the stove or toast in the toaster. Did you watch television or listen to music or use a computer? All of these things required electricity.

Electricity is a kind of natural **energy**. Some people think Benjamin Franklin (1706–1790) or Thomas Edison (1847–1931) invented it. But actually, nobody invented electricity. It's been around since long before humans came along.

Thousands of years ago, people knew about electricity because they could see it in action. Have you ever seen a **lightning** storm? How might people from the ancient past have explained lightning storms?

ESSENTIAL QUESTION

What are some ways electricity is important to our daily lives?

ELECTRICITY

WORDS TO KNOW

electricity: a form of energy caused by the movement of tiny particles. It provides power for lights, appliances, video games, and many other electric devices.

energy: the ability to do things, to work.

lightning: an electrical charge from a cloud.

generate: to create something.

technology: the tools, methods, and systems used to solve a problem or do work.

engineering: the use of science, math, and creativity in the design and construction of things.

static electricity: the buildup of an electric charge on the surface of an object.

BCE: put after a date, BCE stands for Before Common Era and counts down to zero. CE stands for Common Era and counts up from zero. This book was printed in 2022 CE.

amber: a piece of fossilized tree sap or resin.

battery: a device that stores and produces electricity using chemicals.

power: electricity made available to use.

Many of the jobs involved in generating, storing, and using electricity are STEM jobs. STEM is an abbreviation for Science, Technology, Engineering, and Math. You might also hear it referred to as STEAM. The A in STEAM stands for Art and Design.

What about **static electricity**? The ancient Greek scientist Thales of Miletus lived from 625 to 547 **BCE**. He observed that if he rubbed a piece of **amber** with wool or fur, it attracted lightweight objects such as feathers and dust.

What happens when you rub a balloon on your head and stick the balloon to the wall? It stays! We call this static electricity. The ancient Greeks had no name for it.

Ancient peoples found electricity in many different places. Pliny the Elder (23–79), an ancient Greek scientist, observed that being shocked by an electric catfish could help numb a person's pain. Some people even sought this out to help with certain illnesses, such as gout, which causes persistent aches in those who suffer from it. Ancient people didn't know why they felt better after being shocked by an electric fish, but they knew it worked.

Pliny the Elder
Credit: Wellcome Library (CC by 2.0)

THE POWER OF ZAP!

From early times, scientists around the world studied electricity and how it works. But it's been in only the last few hundred years that we've learned how to harness the power of electricity and make it useful to us.

Animals (including humans!) carry electricity in their bodies. Some animals are able to use that electricity to hunt for food. The electric ray, which is a kind of fish, has a special muscle that acts like a **battery**. It sends out a shock to stun creatures in the water. **See this hunting method in action in this video. How might the fish's environment make this method of hunting possible?**

🔎 Vanderbilt electric eel

ELECTRICITY TODAY

Our modern-day lives depend on electricity. Think about the last time you lost **power** at your home. What was it like? Did you have to cook on a grill outside instead of on the electric stove or in your microwave? What did you do for entertainment when your phone and laptop batteries ran out? Did the food in your refrigerator spoil? Lights, computers, televisions, phones, toys, refrigerators—our world revolves electricity.

Sharks have special electrical senses that help them find a tasty fish snack from miles away.

ELECTRICITY

WORDS TO KNOW

blackout: a loss of power.

power grid: a system of power plants and circuits.

outlet: a device in a wall that an electric cord plugs into.

appliance: an electric machine used in the home, such as a toaster or washing machine.

engineer: a person who uses science, math, and creativity to design and build things.

electrical engineer: an engineer who designs systems and processes that use electricity.

physicist: a scientist who studies how matter and energy behave within the universe.

electromagnetism: magnetism created by an electric current.

neurologist: a doctor who studies and cares for the human nervous system.

electrician: a person who installs, fixes, or maintains electric wiring systems.

conductor: something that electricity moves through easily, such as copper wire.

insulator: a material that prevents heat, sound, or electricity from passing through it easily.

circuit: a loop that starts and finishes at the same place.

motor: a machine that turns electric energy into motion.

generator: a device that turns motion into electricity.

We can lose power when storms or other forces knock down electric wires or equipment or when too many people are trying to use electricity at the same time. The biggest **blackout** in the world occurred on July 31, 2012, when 640 million people in India lost power. That's about 10 percent of the world's population! Traffic was a mess without traffic lights, construction projects across the country were halted, and doctors couldn't perform surgeries.

Even our own muscles, including our hearts, rely on electric signals within the body to work!

Experts believe that poor equipment plus high demand for electricity stressed the systems to the point of failure. The country is still working to improve and maintain its **power grid**.

A partial blackout in Brazil
Credit: Diego Torres Silvestre (CC BY 2.0)

THE POWER OF ZAP!

Safety First

Electricity is incredibly important to our lives, and the way it works is fascinating. But it can also be very dangerous. Coming in contact with even a small amount of flowing electricity can burn or even kill. This is because it can disrupt the electric signals our bodies need to work properly. Always treat **outlets**, plugs, and electric **appliances** with care. And remember, the activities in this book are safe as they are written. Don't be tempted to change them.

Engineers are people who use science and math to design and build things. **Electrical engineers** are people who deal with the technology of electricity. But many other people work with and need to understand electricity in their jobs. For example, **physicists** study how things such as **electromagnetism** affect the world. Doctors called **neurologists** study the electrical signals in our bodies. And, of course, **electricians** work with electricity to keep our homes and schools powered.

The word *electricity* comes from the ancient Greek word *elektron*. This was the Greek word for *amber*.

In *Electricity: Circuits, Static, and Electromagnets*, we'll learn what causes electricity and the ways it's generated, stored, and used. And we'll learn about the exciting and essential roles it plays in our lives. We'll find out what **conductors** and **insulators** are, how **circuits** work, and the difference between a **motor** and a **generator**. We'll also explore how scientists are trying to generate Earth-friendly electricity and energy resources. Along the way, we'll get to do some fun projects and experiments.

So, get *charged up* and let's explore electricity!

TEXT TO WORLD

Can you come up with solutions to problems caused by having no electricity? Are there other ways to cook? What's your favorite game or activity to do when the lights are out?

ELECTRICITY

Good Engineering Practices

Every good electrical engineer keeps a science journal! In the first activity, you will make a notebook to use as a design journal. Engineers use the engineering design process to keep track of their inventions, and scientists use the scientific method to keep track of experiments.

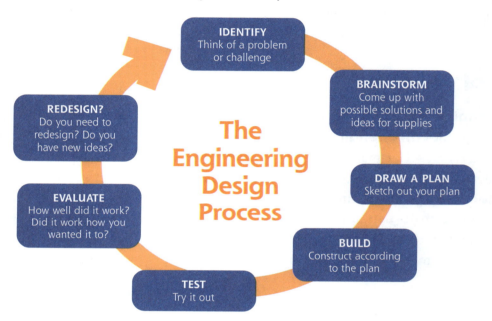

The Engineering Design Process

- **IDENTIFY** Think of a problem or challenge
- **BRAINSTORM** Come up with possible solutions and ideas for supplies
- **DRAW A PLAN** Sketch out your plan
- **BUILD** Construct according to the plan
- **TEST** Try it out
- **EVALUATE** How well did it work? Did it work how you wanted it to?
- **REDESIGN?** Do you need to redesign? Do you have new ideas?

As you read through this book and do the activities, record your observations, data, and designs in an engineering design worksheet or a scientific method worksheet. When doing an activity, remember that there is no right answer or right way to approach an obstacle. Be creative and have fun!

Each chapter of this book begins with an essential question to help guide your exploration of electricity. Keep the question in your mind as you read the chapter. At the end of each chapter, use your science journal to record your thoughts and answers.

> **ESSENTIAL QUESTION**
>
> What are some ways electricity is important to our daily lives?

CREATE YOUR OWN
SCIENCE JOURNAL

Thales of Miletus (circa 624–548 BCE), an ancient Greek scientist, did simple experiments involving electricity. But we know this only because other people wrote about it. None of Thales' writings survived. Make sure your own science journal that looks like an electric outlet to record observations and take notes.

TOOL KIT
- black construction paper
- ruler
- pencil
- a quarter
- 8½ x 11-inch cardstock
- hole punch
- blank paper
- 3 paper brads

❯ **On the black construction paper, use the ruler and pencil to make four rectangles that are 2¼-inches long and ¾-inch wide.** Trace a circle the size of the quarter. Cut out all of the pieces. Next, cut the circle into two equal semi-circles.

❯ **Lay one piece of the cardstock vertically.** Using two of the rectangles and one of the semi-circles, create an outlet near the top of the cardstock. Using the remaining rectangles and semi-circle, create a second outlet near the bottom of the cardstock. Glue all the pieces of black construction paper onto the cardstock and let dry. This will be your journal's cover.

❯ **Sandwich the blank paper between the sheets of cardstock.** The number of pages your journal will have is up to you. You can always add more later. Make sure the pieces of paper and the covers all line up.

❯ **Use the hole punch to punch three evenly spaced holes along the left side of your journal.** Place a paper brad in each hole to bind the journal together. Now, you're ready to *charge* ahead!

Try This!

A scientific method worksheet is a useful tool for keeping your ideas and observations organized. The scientific method is the way scientists ask questions and then find answers. Use the inside pages to make a scientific method worksheet for each experiment.

Question: What are we trying to find out? What problem are we trying to solve?

Research: What is already known about this topic?

Hypothesis: What do we think the answer will be?

Equipment: What supplies are we using?

Method: What procedure are we following?

Results: What happened and why?

WORDS TO KNOW

circa: around that year. Abbreviated with a "c."

vertical: straight up and down.

SWITCH IT UP
EXPERIMENT

TOOL KIT
- science journal
- timer

How many times a day do you use electricity? This experiment is a way to get a sense of how much you rely on electricity without even realizing it.

▶ **To begin, make a prediction about how many times you turn something on or off in one hour.** This can mean flipping a switch, pushing a button, turning a knob, or pulling on a cord. Record your prediction in a scientific method worksheet in your journal.

▶ **Next, set the timer for one hour.** Go about your normal routine. Each time you turn something on or off, make a mark in your journal. These marks will be your data, or scientific results.

▶ **When an hour is up, compare your prediction with your data.** Based on your observations, how much do you rely on electricity?

▶ **Does your environment effect how much electricity you use?** Make a prediction and try the experiment again while you're at school, a store, or the park. Test your prediction and record your data in your journal.

Try This!

Today, there are many types of switches. For example: push button, toggle (these are the one most commonly used), pull-chain or cord, rocker (flat plates that "rock" back and forth), and dimmer. What kind of light switches are in your home? Observe and record your findings in your science journal.

Who Invented the Light Switch?

The first "quick break" light switch was invented in 1884 by John Henry Holmes (1857–1935), an English electrical engineer. Before this, electricity would **arc** when a switch was turned on or off. This means electricity would flow through the air between conductors. This was dangerous and caused damage to switches. Holmes figured out how to move the conductors apart more quickly, eliminating the arc and making the switches safer to use!

WORDS TO KNOW

arc: a curved path, sometimes made by electricity jumping from one thing to another.

Chapter 1

STATIC
ELECTRICITY

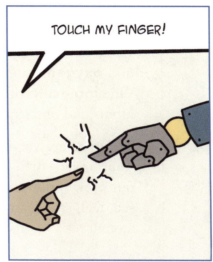

Electricity is all around us. We use it every day, whether we're at home, at school, or in the car. It's hard to imagine a day without electricity. But what, exactly, is electricity? The simple answer is that electricity is a form of energy caused by the movement of **particles** of **matter** called **electrons**. But what are electrons?

Electrons are particles found in **atoms**. Everything in the universe is made up of atoms. These atoms combine in different ways to make trees, computers, the air, animals, rocks—everything, including you!

ESSENTIAL QUESTION

What are some ways we can see or experience static electricity?

WORDS TO KNOW

particle: a tiny piece of matter.

matter: anything that has weight and takes up space.

electron: a negatively charged particle in an atom, part of a shell moving around the center of an atom.

atom: a small particle of matter. Atoms are the extremely tiny building blocks of everything.

9

ELECTRICITY

WORDS TO KNOW

hydrogen: the most common element in the universe, and one of the elements of water.

oxygen: a colorless gas found in the air, needed by animals and humans to breathe.

molecule: a group of atoms bound together. Molecules combine to form matter.

proton: a positively charged particle in the nucleus of an atom.

neutron: a particle inside the nucleus of an atom that has no charge.

electric charge: an amount of stored electricity caused by an imbalance of electrons, either too many or not enough. The electrons flow to fix the imbalance.

neutral: not having a positive or negative charge.

repel: to force away or apart.

nucleus: the center of an atom, made up of protons and neutrons. The plural is nuclei.

ion: an atom that has either fewer electrons than protons or more electrons than protons, and thus has a positive or negative electric charge.

shell: the area around a nucleus through which electrons move.

ELECTRONS AND ELECTRICITY

Some things, such as gold or aluminum, are made of one kind of atom. But most things are made of combinations of atoms. Have you heard water called H_2O? This refers to the combination of **hydrogen** and **oxygen** atoms that make up water. One **molecule** of water has two hydrogen atoms and one oxygen atom.

Atoms are very small bits of matter. They are so small we can't see them with our eyes. But everything we can touch, see, feel, smell, and taste is made of atoms.

Atoms are made of three basic parts—**protons**, **neutrons**, and electrons. Each part of an atom has an **electric charge**, which is either a positive, negative, or **neutral**.

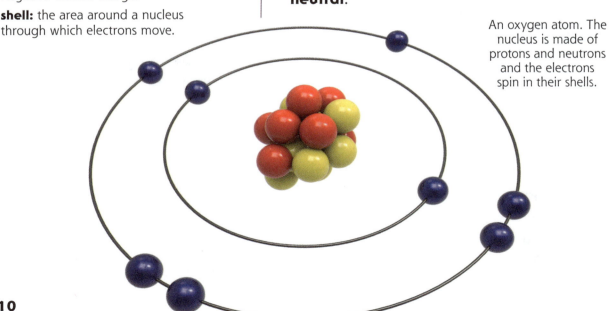

An oxygen atom. The nucleus is made of protons and neutrons and the electrons spin in their shells.

10

STATIC ELECTRICITY

A Hair-Raising Experience

Think back to a dry, cold day when you brushed your hair with a plastic brush or comb or came in from outside and pulled off a wool hat. What happened? Your hair probably stood up straight.

When you combed your hair or pulled off your hat, some electrons rubbed off onto your hair. The hairs on your head all became charged the same way with electrons. And when objects have the same charge, they **repel** each other. The result is a funny, stick-up-everywhere hairdo as your hairs try to get as far away from each other as possible!

Protons and neutrons are in the center of an atom, called the **nucleus**. Protons are small particles with positive electric charges. Neutrons have no electric charge. Electrons are located outside the nucleus. They have negative electric charges—and they are always moving! However, each electron moves only in a specific area, called a **shell**. Within their assigned shells, electrons constantly spin. They move up, down, and sideways.

An atom that gains or loses an electron and has a positive or negative charge is called an ion.

In an atom, the positive charge of one proton cancels out the negative charge of one electron. If the atom has an equal number of protons and electrons, it is neutral with no electric charge.

Different kinds of atoms have different numbers of these positive, negative, and neutral particles. Most of the time, atoms have the same number of electrons as protons.

Check out these science experiments that use static electricity!
What makes balloons stick to the wall (besides tape)?
🔎 Science World static

11

ELECTRICITY

WORDS TO KNOW

humid: having a high level of moisture in the air.

attract: to pull together.

electrostatics: the study of electric charges that are not moving.

magnet: any material that attracts metal.

disc: a round, thin piece of material.

The equal numbers of negative and positive charges are in balance, or neutral. But sometimes, atoms rub against each other and electrons "jump," or move, from atom to atom. This jump causes a stream. And this stream is what we call electricity.

Have you ever gotten a shock from a door handle after walking across a carpet? That's static electricity! Static electricity is caused by the buildup of an electric charge on the surface of an object. When you walk across the carpet, you are building up an electric charge. When you touch a doorknob (or even another person!), the electric charge jumps to the surface of the object you touch with an opposite charge so that both surfaces go back to neutral.

More static electricity builds up on dry days. When the air is humid, the moisture in the air coats the surface of objects and makes it harder for an electric charge to build up. Electricity can travel through water particles, so the electric charge doesn't hang around. But if it's very dry, the electricity has nowhere to go and a static charge builds up.

When objects have opposite charges, they **attract** and move toward each other. Have you ever taken clothes made of different materials out of the dryer? Did they cling together? All that spinning causes some clothes to lose electrons and others to gain them. When you pull the two things apart, the electrons jump and you get a tiny spark and zap.

A Van de Graaff generator is a machine that helps demonstrate **electrostatics**. You've probably seen one at a science museum—it's the machine that causes people's hair to stand straight up when they touch it! **Learn more about Van de Graaff generators here.**

🔎 Van de Graaff MagLab

EXPERIMENTS WITH STATIC ELECTRICITY

Electricity has fascinated thinkers and scientists since ancient times when people observed lightning shoot across the sky.

A few hundred years ago, scientists began studying and experimenting with static electricity. One of these scientists was William Gilbert (1544–1603). Gilbert was a doctor in England who studied the role of **magnets** in electricity. He invented a machine called a versorium. This machine had a wooden pointer that moved toward objects that had been electrically charged by rubbing them with wool or fur.

Later, James Wimshurst (1832–1903) invented the Wimshurst machine, which used turning glass **discs** to create a static electric charge. These charges were then stored in special containers called Leyden jars.

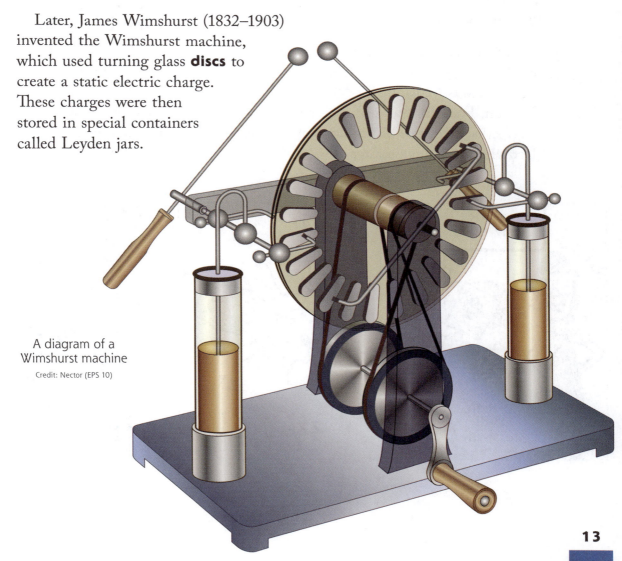

A diagram of a Wimshurst machine
Credit: Nector (EPS 10)

ELECTRICITY

> **WORDS TO KNOW**
>
> **capacitor:** a device that stores electric energy until it's needed.
> **discharge:** the removal of electrons from an object.

Leyden jars, which were named after the place they were invented in Leiden, Netherlands, were early versions of the modern-day **capacitor**. We'll learn more about capacitors later in this book, in Chapter 5.

Because Leyden jars **discharge** their energy all at once, they aren't useful to charge or run things. Like today, they were often used in earlier times for scientific demonstrations or entertainment. For example, some scientists had people hold hands and then sent an electric charge through the entire group!

The part of lightning that comes down from the clouds is called a stepped leader. The part that reaches up from the ground is called a streamer.

One of the most famous people to experiment with electricity was Benjamin Franklin. Franklin was a printer, writer, inventor, and Founding Father of America. Through his experiments, he helped prove that lightning and electricity are the same force.

 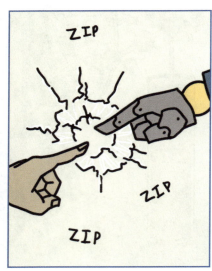 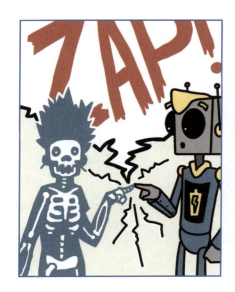

STATIC ELECTRICITY

Reports from Franklin

Ben Franklin described how to conduct his kite experiment in the October 19, 1752, issue of the *Pennsylvania Gazette*.

"This Kite is to be raised when a Thunder Gust appears to be coming on, and the Person who holds the String must stand within a Door, or Window, or under some Cover, so that the Silk Ribbon may not be wet; and Care must be taken that the Twine does not touch the Frame of the Door or Window. As soon as any of the Thunder Clouds come over the Kite, the pointed Wire will draw the Electric Fire from them, and the Kite, with all the Twine, will be electrified, and the loose Filaments of the Twine will stand out every Way, and be attracted by an approaching Finger."

Benjamin Franklin Drawing Electricity from the Sky
Credit: Benjamin West, 1816

 You can read the rest of the account here. How is this different from an account of the actual experience? What kind of details might be missing?

🔍 Founders archives Franklin

15

ELECTRICITY

WORDS TO KNOW

expand: to spread out and take up more space.

interact: when things that are together affect each other.

As the story goes, in 1752, Franklin went out in a thunderstorm and flew a kite with a key tied to the string. The kite's string became charged by the lightning, and when Franklin touched the key, he got a shock. This proved to Franklin that lightning is electricity.

Franklin certainly knew that attracting lightning from a cloud could kill him. So how did he protect himself? Some say he tied a silk ribbon to the end of his kite string. Silk is an insulator, so electricity from lightning moving down the string would have stopped when it hit the ribbon. But this was incredibly risky. You should never try this dangerous experiment yourself!

LIGHTNING

During a storm, wind moves around the clouds, which are made up of water droplets. Most lightning occurs when a negative charge builds up toward the bottom of the cloud. When the charge gets too great, the cloud tries to get rid of some of it.

The ground is positively charged because the negative charge of the cloud forces the negative charges in the ground away from the surface. Sometimes, the charges are reversed—the ground is negatively charged and the cloud is positively charged. But the results are the same.

Lightning is one of the most powerful, beautiful, and dangerous examples of static electricity.

So, as the negative charge from the cloud moves down, the opposite positive charge from the ground or tall objects, such as buildings and trees, moves up. The two charges meet in the middle and lightning strikes!

But all of this happens so fast that our brains think the lightning is only moving downward.

16

STATIC ELECTRICITY

What usually goes along with lightning? Thunder! All that movement of charges causes a lot of heat. Lightning is very hot, around 50,000 degrees Fahrenheit (27,760 degrees Celsius). That's about five times hotter than the sun. The heat causes the air to **expand** quickly. That rapid expansion of air causes a noise and that's why we hear thunder.

Most of the time, lightning doesn't reach the ground. It just moves from cloud to cloud. These are called cloud flashes. They happen when a negatively charged cloud meets up with a positively charged cloud. Ever heard the term "opposites attract?" It's true in the case of lightning!

You can estimate how close a thunderstorm is by counting. Count the number of seconds after you see a lightning flash and when you hear thunder. Divide that number by five and that's about how many miles away the storm is.

There are other types of lightning, as well. For instance, cloud-to-air. This happens when positively charged air particles in a cloud are attracted to negatively charged air particles. And intracloud lightning happens when differently charged areas within a single cloud **interact**.

17

ELECTRICITY

WORDS TO KNOW

resistance: a force that slows down another force.

You might hear of something called heat lightning, too. It's called this because it's usually associated with summertime storms. This isn't a specific type of lightening, though. Instead, it's lightning you can see from a storm you can't hear. This happens when a thunderstorm is far away. As humans, we can see a storm from much farther away than we can hear it.

When lightning does reach the ground, the consequences can be deadly. Every year, lightning kills about 70 people in the United States. And many houses and buildings are hit and catch fire.

Does static electricity serve a useful purpose? Yes! Printers and copiers use static electricity to attract the ink to the paper. Paint sprayers and air filters use it, too!

As we learned earlier, lightning always looks for the easiest path to travel, or the path of least **resistance**. Tall objects offer that easy path.

Stay Safe Around Lightning

Lightning storms can be very dangerous. Here are some ways to keep yourself safe.

> If you can hear thunder, head inside. Lightning can strike from 10 miles away.

> If you're outside in a storm and the hairs on your arm stick up, find shelter immediately. It may mean the ground is building up a positive charge—and you're a part of that positive charge.

> Don't take shelter under a tree. Trees are usually the tallest thing around. They give lightning the easiest path to the ground, so they attract lightning.

> If you can't get indoors or into a shelter, crouch down near the ground with your head tucked and hands over your ears.

STATIC ELECTRICITY

Stop the Zaps

Static electricity can give us tiny shocks. You may not be able to avoid those zaps all the time, but here are a few simple ways you can cut back on the number of times they happen.

If it's not too cold, go barefoot inside your house. When socks and rubber-soled shoes rub against carpet, a static electric charge can build up. You can also wear leather-soled shoes.

Choose cotton clothes. Wool and synthetic fabrics such as polyester and nylon are good conductors of electricity.

Ask your parents about running a humidifier in your house in the winter. More static electricity builds up in dry air. A humidifier is a device that adds moisture to the air.

Use dryer sheets (which help balance electrons in clothes). You can also rub a dryer sheet on your carpet to help.

Use moisturizer so you don't have dry skin, which can increase your chances of being shocked.

Touch a metal object every now and then to help dispel built-up electric charges.

An illustration from the book *A History of Electricity: The Intellectual Rise in Electricity from Antiquity to the Days of Benjamin Franklin* by Park Benjamin, 1898

ELECTRICITY

WORDS TO KNOW

lightning rod: a rod or pole used to move the electric charge from lightning safely into the ground.

efficient: wasting as little as possible.

Most tall buildings have a pointed metal rod or pole attached to the roof as protection from a lightning strike. These are called **lightning rods** and were invented by Benjamin Franklin.

A lightning rod connects to a huge piece of copper or aluminum wire. Both copper and aluminum are good conductors of electricity. The tall rod provides an easy path for the massive electric currents from lightning to travel safely to the ground and away from the building.

Check out a simulation of a lightning rod doing its job during a storm! How does the intensity of the lightning bolt affect the rod's effectiveness?

🔍 lightning rod simulator

As we've learned, static electricity can be shockingly fun. Now, let's learn how we can use and harness electricity in other ways.

Two Strikes and You're . . .

Have you ever heard the saying, "Lightning never strikes twice in the same place?" Well, it's not true! Lightning is very **efficient** and always looks for the quickest path to the ground. This is the path of lowest resistance. A tall, wet object is less resistant to lightning than the air. So tall buildings can, and often do, get hit over and over. The Empire State Building in New York City is hit by lightning about 100 times a year. Luckily, it has lightning rods.

ESSENTIAL QUESTION

What are some ways we can see or experience static electricity?

BOOGIE BALLS BOX

In the eighteenth century, people used static electricity to entertain. For example, Stephen Gray (1666–1736) performed "The Flying Boy." In this demonstration, a young boy was suspended on silk cords and his feet were charged with a special ball. The static electricity would travel through his body and he could use it to turn the pages of a book without touching them! Here's a fun way to entertain your friends and family.

BBC Stephen gray

TOOL KIT
- shoebox lid
- foil
- pencil
- 5 small Styrofoam balls about the size of large marbles
- 8-by-10-inch polycarbonate sheet (Plexiglass), found at hardware stores
- dry paper towel
- science journal

▶ **Lay the shoebox lid on top of a piece of foil.** Trace around it with the pencil. Carefully cut out the piece of foil and lay it in the bottom of the lid.

▶ **Cover each of the Styrofoam balls with foil.** Smooth them out the best you can so that they are round and smooth. Place the balls inside the lid.

▶ **Use the paper towel to rub one side of the polycarbonate sheet for 20 to 30 seconds.** (Important: The sheet usually comes with a clear film on each side. Be sure to peel off the film before rubbing.) This will "charge" the polycarbonate sheet with static electricity.

▶ **Place the polycarbonate sheet over the lid, rubbed-side down.** The sheet doesn't need to completely cover the lid, but it should be close to the tops of the foil balls without touching them. Observe and record what happens to the foil-covered balls underneath. Glide your finger along the top of the plastic sheet. The balls should hover, move, or "dance." Note that if the foil on the bottom of the lid pulls up, you might have to glue or tape it down.

Try This!

What happens if you add five more foil-covered Styrofoam balls? Does the charge last for the same amount of time? Are the balls just as active?

What happens if you don't cover the balls in foil?

What happens if you rub the polycarbonate sheet for only five seconds?

What happens if your paper towel is damp?

Make predictions, experiment, and record your data in your science journal.

21

MAKE AN
ELECTROSCOPE

William Gilbert used a device called a versorium to test an object's electric charge. You can make a similar device called an electroscope to see static electricity at work. An electroscope can detect electric charges.

> **❱ Flip the jar over onto the cardboard.** Use a pencil to trace around the top. Cut out the circle. This will be your jar's lid.

> **❱ Straighten the paper clip until it looks like the letter L.** Carefully poke the paper clip into the middle of the cardboard lid and slide it through until about 1½ inches of the top of the L is above the lid. The part with the right angle will be on the bottom.

> **❱ Form a small piece of modeling clay into flat shape.** Mold it on top of the lid around the wire to keep the wire in place.

> **❱ Crumble a piece of aluminum foil into a ball that's a little bit smaller than a golf ball.** Push it onto the wire that's above the lid. Be careful not to let the ball touch the cardboard.

> **❱ Cut a piece of foil that is 3½ inches by a ½ inch.** Fold it in half and drape it over the bent part of the wire so that it hangs below the lid. Use a small drop of glue under the fold to hold the foil in place.

TOOL KIT
° medium glass jar
° cardboard
° large, metal paper clip
° modeling clay
° aluminum foil
° ruler
° white glue
° tape
° balloon
° wool blanket
° science journal

Try This!

Create a scientific method worksheet with a list of other things in your house that might have an electric charge. Test them out with your electroscope. Record your data in your science journal.

WORDS TO KNOW

electroscope: a device that is able to detect electric charges.

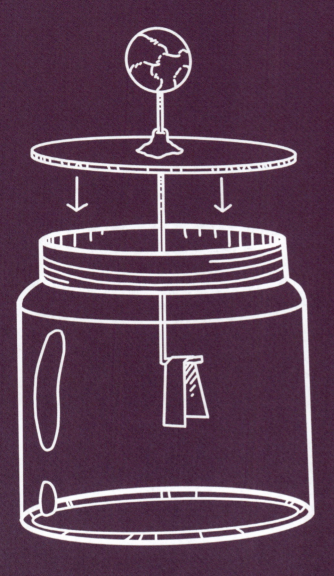

❯ **Carefully place the lid on the jar.** The foil flaps should be inside the jar. The foil ball should be on the outside. Use tape to attach the lid to the jar.

❯ **Try out your electroscope!** Blow up the balloon and rub it on the wool blanket for about 30 seconds. Hold the balloon close to the foil ball above your jar. What happens to the foil flaps inside the jar?

Consider This!

The aluminum flaps should move apart because the static electricity is moving from the balloon into the foil ball, down the wire, and into the foil flaps. The flaps have the same charge, so they are trying to move away from each other.

TEXT TO WORLD

Why is it important to be able to detect electric charges? Can you think of some jobs where it would be helpful and safer if you knew if and how much electricity was around?

23

STATIC ELECTRICITY
IN ACTION

TOOL KIT
- 6-inch piece of string
- 2 identical plastic straws
- tape
- table or cabinet
- paper towel

The ancient Greeks didn't understand what caused static electricity, but they could see it. You can see it, too, with a few easy-to-find items.

❯ **Tie the string around the middle of one of the straws.** Tape the string to the edge of a table so the straw hangs **horizontally.**

❯ **Rub the straw all over with the paper towel.** Make sure to keep the straw in a horizontal position.

❯ **Rub the second straw with the paper towel.** Slowly bring the side of the second straw toward the hanging straw. What happens and why? Create a scientific method worksheet in your journal and write down your ideas.

❯ **Predict what will happen if you move the paper towel toward the hanging straw.** Try it. What happens? Record your observations in your journal.

Consider This!

When you rub the straws with the towel, you give them the same charge. Then, when you put the straws close together, they repel one another. The paper towel has an opposite charge, so the hanging straw is attracted to it.

Try This!

Is static electricity strong enough to move water? Find out! Turn the faucet on to produce a small but steady stream of water. Next, use the paper towel to rub the straw. Count to 20 slowly while you do it. Now, slowly bring the side of the straw toward the water. Look carefully. What's happening? Write or draw what you see.

WORDS TO KNOW

horizontal: straight from side to side.

Chapter 2

CURRENTS

It's easy to find examples of static electricity all around us, from lightning to the static electricity we can create on our own bodies. But what about the electricity that keeps the lights on and powers our **electronic** devices?

With static electricity, electrons build up and stay where they are until they touch another object and jump over. With **dynamic electricity**, electrons are always moving. And this constant motion creates an **electric current**, or a stream of charged particles, and that's what we use to power our lives.

> **ESSENTIAL QUESTION**
>
> How is the electricity we use to power things such as appliances different from static electricity?

WORDS TO KNOW

electronic: describes a device that uses computer parts to control the flow of electricity.

dynamic electricity: the movement of an electric charge through a conductor.

electric current: the flow of an electric charge through a conductor.

25

ELECTRICITY

WORDS TO KNOW

electrocution: to be injured or killed by electricity.

grounded: a circuit in which the current flows directly into the ground.

You might think of it like water flowing from a faucet to the end of a garden hose when you turn the spigot. Electricity also moves from one point to another. Instead of traveling through a hose, electricity travels along materials that are good conductors. And when we flip a switch, we're simply creating a path for that current.

CONDUCTORS AND INSULATORS

Electricity always takes the easiest path. It's the most efficient way to travel! Some materials allow an electric current to move through them easily. These are called conductors. Metals such as silver, gold, copper, aluminum, brass, iron, and steel are all excellent conductors. So are people, animals, and water.

Other materials don't allow electricity to move through them easily. These are called insulators. Good insulators include glass, rubber, plastic, diamonds, and air. Insulators protect us from **electrocution**. When conductors and insulators are used together, electricity can be used as safely as possible.

Copper is an excellent conductor.

CURRENTS

Check out the cords on the appliances in your house. You'll see a plastic covering on the outside. If you could look inside the plastic covering, you'd see a wire. (Remember: Don't cut the cord to look.) When you plug the cord into an outlet on the wall, an electric current moves along the wire into the appliance. The plastic covering on the cord makes it safe to handle anything that needs to be plugged in.

BIRDS ON A WIRE

Have you ever seen a line of birds settled on a power line? Shouldn't they should find a safer place to sit?! But birds can stand on power lines and not get hurt.

Why is that? Electricity always wants to move from a high charge to a low charge. Imagine the electrons are at a party and think, "It's too crowded here. I'm going to where it's less crowded." And the lowest-charged place around is the ground, not the bird. But what if the bird, or any living creature, touches a power line and the ground—or something else in contact with the ground—at the same time?

Then it becomes a pathway for the electricity. The object touching the power line is said to be **grounded**, and the electricity now has an efficient way to travel from power line to the ground.

If a living thing becomes a pathway for electricity, it is electrocuted. Electrocution often leaves a victim severely burned or even dead. This is because our hearts and other body parts use electric pulses. If those are interrupted by a high amount of outside electricity, the heart's rhythm can change or stop.

ELECTRICITY

WORDS TO KNOW

pressure: a force that pushes on an object.

voltage: the force, measured in volts, that moves electrons in an electric current.

potential energy: the amount of energy that is possible.

superconductor: a material that can carry electricity without resistance.

magnetic resonance imaging (MRI) machine: a machine used to see inside the body.

magnetic levitation: the use of magnetic fields generated by superconducting magnets to cause an object (such as a vehicle) to float above a solid surface.

amperes (amps): the measurement of the amount of electric current.

Because water is an excellent conductor of electricity, always keep electric items away from water. Never bring electric devices into the bathtub! And never go near water during a lightning storm.

What about the people who work on power lines? Aren't they touching the ground? They are, but people who work on power lines are trained to work with electricity. They wear special boots and gloves and use buckets that are insulated. They also use special tools that protect them from the dangers of their job.

VOLTS, AMPS, AND WATTS

When we talk about electric current, we use certain words to describe and measure it. Let's think about that garden hose again. When you turn on the spigot, you usually don't have to wait for the water. It starts moving down the hose right away. That's because there is **pressure** on the water as it goes through the pipes to reach the hose. When the water valve is opened—swoosh! The pressure is released and water flows.

The flow of electricity works the same way. A force called **voltage** makes electrons flow. Voltage is measured in volts. A higher voltage means more pressure. And this means more **potential energy**.

Batteries can supply this kind of force. Most of the batteries you find in your house produce only about 1.5 volts. That's not a very high potential to do work. That's why batteries don't hurt you. You can open the back of a television remote control and pop out the batteries without feeling any kind of zap. Batteries in use can get very warm, though, so still be careful.

CURRENTS

Superconductors!

When some materials are cooled way down to hundreds of degrees below zero Fahrenheit, they can carry electricity perfectly. This means there's no resistance to the flow. Instead of bumping into each other, the electrons all move together in sync. These materials are called **superconductors**. Some examples of superconductors are aluminum, mercury, niobium, and magnesium diboride. Superconductors are useful in many ways. **Magnetic resonance imaging (MRI) machines** are made possible by superconductors. So are trains that use **magnetic levitation** to move along tracks at very high speed. Superconductors are used in particle accelerators, also called colliders, which are powerful machines scientists use to study atom particles.

A regular wall outlet has far more potential power than a 1.5-volt battery. Its 120 volts is enough force to give you a powerful shock. The voltage is different in other countries. Often, it's much higher than the voltage in the United States. This is because they use different systems or decided higher voltage was cheaper.

You should never stick anything inside an outlet other than a plug. You might find plastic plugs in outlets that aren't in use in homes with babies and young children. The plastic plugs prevent a child from sticking a toy or fork into a socket and getting electrocuted.

In an electric current, electrons move very quickly from atom to atom. The number of electrons that move past a point during a certain amount of time is measured in units called **amperes**, or amps. Think of rivers flowing. A large river and a small river may travel at the same rate, but more water flows in a large river. A higher number of amps means more electricity is flowing.

A wire carrying one amp has about 6,250,000,000,000,000,000 electrons flowing across it per second.

ELECTRICITY

WORDS TO KNOW

climate change: the long-term change in the earth's weather patterns.

wattage: the amount of power, measured in watts, that's created or used.

dissect: to cut something apart to study what is inside.

nerve: a fiber that transmits messages from the brain to the body and vice versa.

In 2017, Tesla, an American automotive and energy company, built the world's largest lithium-ion, rechargeable battery in South Australia. **Learn more in this video. What role do batteries play in plans to combat climate change?**

🔍 Tesla battery Australia

The standard in houses in the United States is between 100 and 200 amps. Some houses may have less or more, depending on their size or electrical systems. And different items use different amps. For example, a refrigerator uses between three and 15 amps, a microwave uses about 10 amps, and a phone charger uses around one amp.

Volts and amps together equal power to do work. That amount of power is called **wattage**, which is measured in watts. Watts measure how much energy is released per second. To go back to our previous examples, a typical refrigerator is between 350 and 780 watts, a microwave is 500 to 1,500 watts, and a phone charger is about five watts. To figure out how much power is available, scientists use the formula *amps x volts = watts*.

WHY WOULD YOU NEED A COMPLETELY NEW BATTERY?

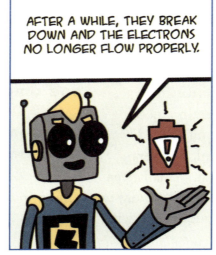
AFTER A WHILE, THEY BREAK DOWN AND THE ELECTRONS NO LONGER FLOW PROPERLY.

WELL, WE BETTER GO GET YOU A NEW BATTERY THEN!

CURRENTS

DID A FROG HELP INVENT THE BATTERY?

Batteries are one source of electric current. Batteries are very important in our daily lives! Think about how many devices rely on batteries for power. Who invented the battery and how does it work?

A teacher in Italy named Luigi Galvani (1737–1798) **dissected** frogs to study their bodies. One night, the scissors he was using touched the **nerves** in the frog's legs and the dead frog's legs moved! Nerves are special pathways between the body and the brain. Galvani thought the frog's legs moved because they had electricity running through them. He called this "animal electricity."

Galvani's drawings of his experiments
Credit: Wellcome Gallery (CC BY 4.0)

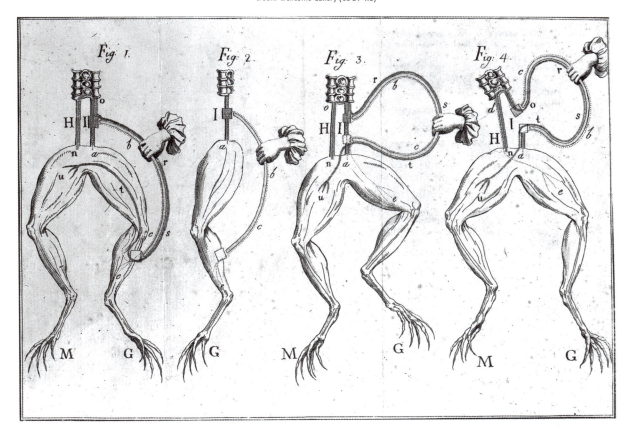

31

ELECTRICITY

WORDS TO KNOW

theory: an idea that could explain how or why something happens.

cell: in a battery, a single unit of a battery made up of an anode and a cathode that are separated by an electrolyte.

chemical reaction: the rearrangement of atoms in a substance to make a new chemical substance.

electrode: a conductor through which electricity enters and leaves an object, such as a battery.

electrolyte: a liquid or paste in a battery that allows for the flow of electric current.

anode: the end of a battery marked with a minus sign.

cathode: the end of a battery marked with a plus sign.

fossil fuel: a source of energy that comes from the fossils of plants and animals that lived millions of years ago. These include coal, oil, and natural gas.

Another Italian teacher named Alessandro Volta (1745–1827) heard about this, but he had a different **theory**. He thought the frog's legs jumped because of the metal tools Galvani used. Volta decided to test his idea. He began by stacking different metal discs on top of each other. But when he touched them, nothing happened. There was no charge. Then he soaked a piece of cardboard in salt water and put it between zinc and copper discs. These units, called **cells**, did produce a small charge.

Next, Volta stacked many cells on top of each other, each separated by a layer of cardboard soaked in salt water. When he touched the stack, he got a huge shock!

What was happening? Volta had unknowingly built the first simple battery!

A **chemical reaction** between molecules in the materials Volta used caused electrons to move. The salt water was a great conductor. A regular battery, such as the kind you find in a flashlight, works in a similar way. It has two metal plates called **electrodes** at the ends of the battery.

An **electrolyte** connects the electrodes. The **anode** is the flat metal plate on one end and is marked as the negative end.

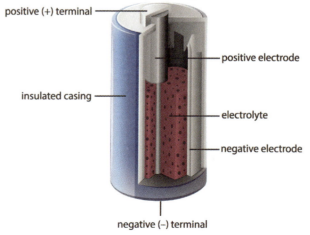

Parts of a Dry Cell
- positive (+) terminal
- positive electrode
- insulated casing
- electrolyte
- negative electrode
- negative (–) terminal

32

CURRENTS

The **cathode** is marked as the positive end and always has a bump on it. The cathode and anode are made of different metals.

When a battery is hooked up to a device such as a flashlight, a chemical reaction starts inside. The electrolyte includes ions that carry electrons from the cathode to the anode. This causes the anode to have more electrons. The electrons want to be in balance. When a battery is hooked up to an object, the electrons head out of the anode, power the object using electricity, and then travel back to the cathode.

There's more to learn about how we use electricity to power things. For example, how does electricity move? How can we turn it off and on? This is where circuits come in! We'll find out more in the next chapter.

Developing Batteries!

Scientists in the fields of materials science and engineering as well as energy systems and technology are researching, developing, and improving the batteries used in electric or hybrid cars. A hybrid car is one that uses both a **fossil fuel** and electricity.

Electric and hybrid cars use a type of rechargeable battery called a lithium-ion battery. In these types of batteries, lithium ions move through the electrolyte when discharging energy and back again when charging. These batteries are also used in many products such as cell phones, wireless headphones, power tools, watches, electric scooters and wheelchairs, and small appliances. They are lightweight, have a long life, can produce more power than alkaline batteries, and can hold a charge longer than other rechargeable batteries.

But they have some limits, too. For example, lithium-ion batteries aren't strong enough to run large trucks or aircraft. And if they aren't stored or charged properly, they can cause fires or explosions. Lithium-ion batteries are more expensive and have a bigger carbon footprint than other batteries as well.

ESSENTIAL QUESTION

How is the electricity we use to power things such as appliances different from static electricity?

MAKE A
VOLTAIC PILE

Alessandro Volta created the first cell battery. Here's a way to make your own. Note: It's important the pennies you use are dated before 1982 because these coins will have more copper. Also use washers that are **galvanized**, or coated with **zinc**. How can you tell? Galvanized metal is usually dull and non-galvanized metal is usually shiny. The washers may also be labeled as "zinc washers."

TOOL KIT
° 5 pennies dated before 1982
° 2 cotton makeup pads
° 1 tablespoon salt
° 3/8 cup hot water
° 5 3/4-inch galvanized washers
° small rubber band
° 10-mm LED light (rated for 3 volts) available at craft or model stores or online
° science journal

❯ **Using one of the pennies and a pen, trace three circles on one of the makeup pads.** On a second makeup pad, trace two more circles. Cut out the circles.

❯ **Pour the salt into the hot water.** Use a spoon to stir the water until the salt is all dissolved. Carefully wet one of the cotton circles with the salt water. You want it soaked but not dripping. The salt water will be acting as your battery's electrolyte.

❯ **Lay a penny on a flat surface.** Lay the cotton circle soaked with salt water on top of the penny.

❯ **Carefully lay a washer on top of the wet cotton pad.** This will be your first "cell." The pennies and washers are your battery's electrodes. Continue to create cells, one on top of the other: penny, cotton circle soaked in salt water, washer.

❯ **When you have five cells, hold the stack between your thumb and pointer finger.** Carefully wrap the rubber band around the stack (top to bottom) to hold the five cells together.

TEXT TO **WORLD**

What would life be like without batteries? What kinds of activities would be more difficult or impossible?

❱ **Look at your LED.** It should have two wires (or leads) coming down from the bottom. One of these is the positive end and the other is the negative end. Positive leads are usually longer. If you happen to have an LED with legs of the same length, look inside the bottom of the bulb for two metal triangular pieces. The smaller one connects to the positive lead and the bigger one connects to the negative lead.

❱ **Touch the positive lead to the bottom penny and the negative lead to the top washer.** You may have to bend the leads slightly. The LED should light up!

❱ **If your light doesn't glow, there are some things you can try.**

* Make sure you have the correct ends of the LED touching the bottom penny and top washer.

* Dry off the battery cell. If the salt water is dripping, it might be interfering with the flow of electricity.

* Go to a darker area, such as a closet. The LED might be hard to see in brighter light.

* Double check to see if you're using pennies dated before 1982 as well as galvanized washers.

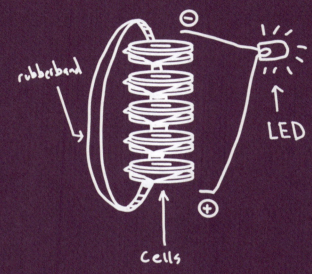

Try This!

What do you think would happen if you used more cells? What about fewer cells? Try it and see. Record your observations in your science journal.

WORDS TO KNOW

galvanized: coated with zinc.

zinc: a chemical element that helps protect iron and steel from damage.

MAKE A
VINEGAR BATTERY

Batteries need an electrolyte to work. In the last project, we used salt water as an electrolyte. This time, we'll use vinegar.

> **TOOL KIT**
> ° ice cube tray (or a recycled Styrofoam egg carton)
> ° vinegar
> ° 20-inch piece of copper wire
> ° wire cutters
> ° 5 galvanized nails
> ° 10 mm LED light (rated for 3 volts)
> ° science journal

❯ **Fill six sections of the ice cube tray or Styrofoam egg carton) with vinegar.** The sections should be about half to three-quarters of the way full of the vinegar.

❯ **Cut the wire into pieces.** You want five, 4-inch pieces.

❯ **Around the top of one nail, wrap an end of one wire and wind the wire tightly around several times.** Bend the rest of the wire so that the nail-wire unit looks like a lowercase letter "n."

❯ **Wrap the remaining nails the same way with the remaining wire.** You should have five letter "n" shaped units.

❯ **Starting in the lower-right corner of the ice cube tray or egg carton, place the nail of one of the nail-wire units into the vinegar.** Place the wire from that nail in the cup of vinegar to the left.

❯ **Place the nail of another nail-wire unit in the cup with the copper wire.** Make sure the nail and wire aren't touching. The wire from that unit should sit in the cup to the left.

❯ **Moving in a counterclockwise direction, add the remaining nail-wire units so that each cup has one nail and one copper wire.** Continue to make sure that the nail and wires are not touching each other inside the vinegar in each section. When you're done, one cup will have a copper wire but no nail. And the cup next to it will have a nail but no copper wire.

What's Happening?

The vinegar creates a pathway for electricity to travel.

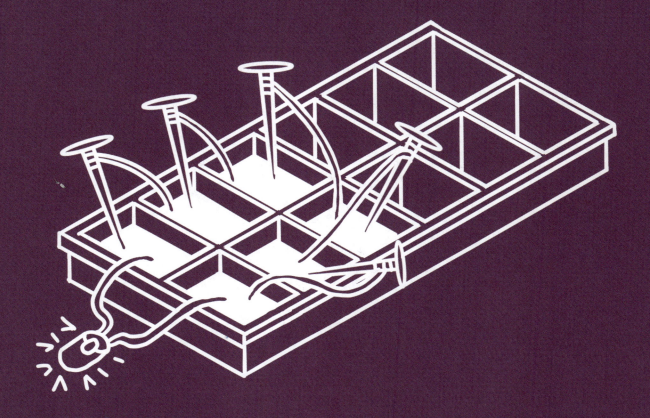

❯ **Place the positive end of the LED light into the cup of vinegar with the copper wire.** What do you think will happen when you place the negative end of the LED into the cup of vinegar with the nail? Write your prediction in your science journal.

❯ **Place the negative end of the LED light into the cup of vinegar with the nail.** What happened? Write down your observations in your science journal.

Try This!

Is there anything special about the vinegar and the salt water from the last experiment? Do you think other types of liquids would work in this experiment? Try a few other liquids and see what happens.

WATTS IN ACTION

A watt is a unit of power. It measures the amount of power generated or the amount used by an electric object. The higher the number of watts, the more power the object has and the more work it can do. Here's a simple way to see this in action.

TOOL KIT
- small balloon
- bigger balloon
- sharp pin
- science journal

❯ **Make two water balloons.** Fill both balloons with water and tie them off.

❯ **Hold the small balloon above the sink.** Carefully poke the bottom of it with the pin. Observe how fast the water comes out. Record your observations in your science journal.

❯ **Hold the bigger balloon over the sink.** Carefully poke the bottom of it with the pin. Observe how fast the water comes out. Record your observation in your science journal.

❯ **Which balloon pushed out the water with more power?** Why do you think that is? Write down your theory in your science journal.

Try This!

How fast would the water come out of different-sized balloons? Fill up various sizes of balloons and repeat the experiment.

What's that "W" stand for?

Look at the top or the base of a light bulb that's not screwed in. You'll see a number followed by a W, for example, 60W. That's the bulb's wattage, or the amount of energy used to make the bulb shine. Watts can also mean the amount of power an electric device needs to run. Appliances have watt numbers on them to tell you that. A typical washing machine uses 500 watts and an electric dryer uses 4,000 watts.

A megawatt is equal to 1,000,000 watts.

Chapter 3

CIRCUITS

Imagine a racetrack. The cars are revving up at the starting line and someone waves the flag. And . . . they're off! As the cars speed around the track, nothing gets in their way. They keep going around and around until someone waves the flag to signal the end of the race.

A traveling path that begins and ends at the same spot is called a circuit. Racetracks are circuits. Do you have a flowing lazy river at your local pool? That's another kind of circuit. Can you think of other circuits you've come across?

Circuits are very useful, especially when it comes to electricity.

> **ESSENTIAL QUESTION**
>
> How does electricity travel across the country and into our homes and businesses?

ELECTRICITY

WORDS TO KNOW

electric circuit: the pathway electricity follows.

switch: a control that opens or closes a circuit.

series circuit: a circuit with a single path from the power source to the load and back to the power source.

load: the object that uses the electricity in a circuit.

FOLLOW THE CIRCUIT

Electricity travels on a path we call an **electric circuit**. In the simplest circuit, electricity moves from a power source through a conductor to an electric device and then back to the power source. In this kind of circuit, electricity is always flowing and the device is always on, which is a good thing if you want your food to stay cold in the refrigerator. That's a device that should always stay on.

What if we want to turn off that flow of electricity?

Most circuits have built-in breaks that we can use to stop the flow of electricity. These breaks are called **switches**. They open and close a circuit. Some examples of this kind of circuit are a lamp, an oven, and computer.

Just like the cars on a racetrack, electricity needs a clear path.

In this series circuit, the battery is the power source, the switch is closed so the electricity can flow, and two electric devices—light bulbs—are lit up with electricity!

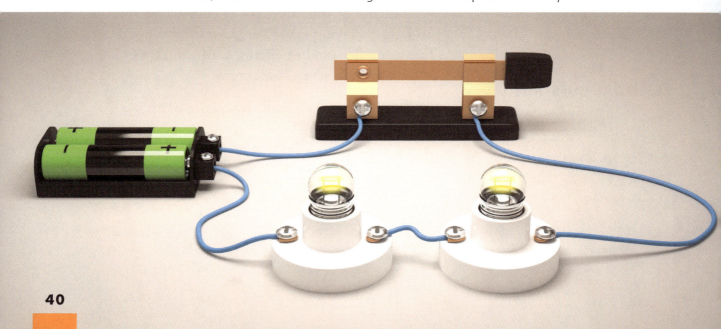

40

CIRCUITS

We use switches all the time to turn things on and off. If nothing is stopping the electrons, the circuit is closed and electricity is flowing. If there's a break in the path, the circuit is open and electrons can't flow through.

Test this with a light switch. What happens when the light is off? Which position is the switch in? And when you turn the light on, is the circuit open or closed?

In a **series circuit**, electricity can travel on only one path. The electricity goes from one **load**—or electronic device—to another, to another, and so on. Think of an old-style string of Christmas tree lights. All the lights rely on the same power source, so if one bulb goes out, the rest do, too—the burned-out bulb opens the circuit.

Circuit Parts

A circuit has four parts.

> A power source, such as a battery or outlet
> A path for the electricity, usually a wire
> The load, or the object that uses the energy in the power source
> A switch

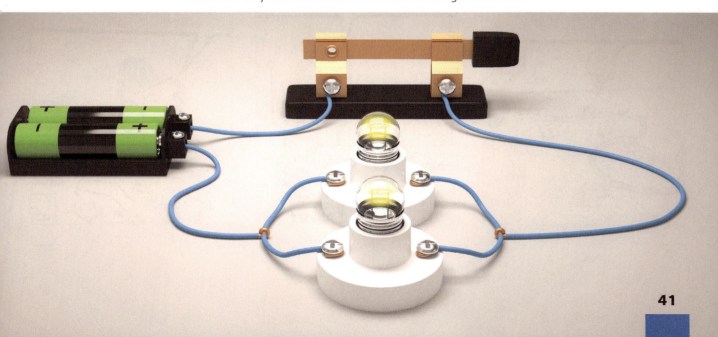

In this parallel circuit, both light bulbs are connected to the power source so they can each burn even if the other light bulb fails.

41

ELECTRICITY

WORDS TO KNOW

parallel circuit: a circuit with a pathway to the power source for each load.

filament: the wire used as the conducting material inside a light bulb.

incandescent: a source of electric light that works by heating a filament.

short circuit: a direct connection between two points in a circuit that aren't supposed to be directly connected.

In a **parallel circuit**, each load has its own pathway back to the power source. These types of circuits are helpful when we need devices to stay on when one load is out. Think of a hallway in your house with two or more lights that the same switch turns on and off. If one light goes out, the rest keep working so you can still find your way around. Many newer strings of holiday lights work this way today.

THE LIGHT BULB

Maybe you've heard that Thomas Edison invented the light bulb. He wasn't the first to do so, but all the bulbs before his burned out after only a few minutes. In earlier bulbs, the metal thread the electricity ran through, called the **filament**, got too hot and burned up quickly. It was also very expensive.

CIRCUITS

In 1879, Edison used cotton thread for the filament, which didn't cost as much. He also decided to take out more of the oxygen from inside the glass bulb. Without oxygen, fire can't burn. Less oxygen meant less chance of the filament burning up. His bulb lasted at least 13 hours!

By 1925, half of all homes in the United States had electric power. The rest still used gaslight and candles. Electricity was attractive because it was cleaner to burn. Plus, it didn't cause as many house fires.

An LED and two CFL light bulbs

Today, we have different kinds of light bulbs. Traditional **incandescent** bulbs use a filament made of a metal called tungsten. Tungsten doesn't melt until it reaches 6,191 degrees Fahrenheit (3,422 degrees Celsius). Each piece of tungsten is about 20 inches long, but it's coiled up tightly so it takes up less space.

Short Circuits

Wires that carry electricity can lose their insulation. If this happens and the wires are too close to one another, the electrons can jump from one wire to the other, causing a **short circuit**. Short circuits can cause power outages and fires. A short circuit is when an electric current follows an unplanned path. It can also happen when a storm or an animal damages a power line and cuts off electricity. Loose connections inside an appliance or electric outlet can also cause short circuits.

ELECTRICITY

WORDS TO KNOW

compact fluorescent light (CFL): a light bulb that uses less electricity and lasts longer than an incandescent light bulb.

ultraviolet light: a kind of light with short wavelengths. It can't be seen with the naked eye.

element: a pure substance that is made of atoms that are all the same.

implement: to put into effect.

halogen bulb: a gas-filled incandescent bulb.

greenhouse gas: a gas in the atmosphere that traps heat and contributes to warming temperatures.

atmosphere: a layer of gas surrounding Earth.

solar: relating to the sun.

light-emitting diode (LED): a light bulb that provides very efficient lighting.

diode: a semiconductor device that allows the flow of current in one direction.

semiconductor: a material that conducts some electricity.

landfill: a place where trash and other waste materials are buried and covered with soil.

Compact fluorescent lights (CFLs) use much less energy than incandescent bulbs to give off the same amount of light. And they last a lot longer. CFLs have no filament at all. Instead, they have spiral-shaped tubes that hold gases, including mercury. The inside of the tubes is coated with a white powder called phosphor. When electricity runs through the bulb, the mercury heats up. It gives off a special kind of light called **ultraviolet light**, which causes the phosphor to glow brightly.

CFLs have some challenges. For example, they are sensitive to cold temperatures. They also contain mercury, a chemical **element** that's harmful to people and the environment, which makes them hard to dispose of safely.

The Light Bulb Debate

The U.S. Federal Light Bulb Efficiency Standard, **implemented** in 2007 and signed into law in 2017, sought to require all light bulbs to become more efficient by 2020. Many stores began phasing out incandescent and **halogen bulbs** to make room for the more energy-efficient LED bulbs. And people got used to buying the new technology. But in late 2019, the U.S. Department of Energy decided to reverse the standards, saying that people should be able to choose what kind of light bulbs they want to use. What do you think?

CIRCUITS

Saving the Planet

If every American home replaced just one incandescent light bulb with an LED bulb, it could reduce the **greenhouse gases** going into the **atmosphere** by the equivalent of 550,000 cars! Although LED bulbs are more expensive to buy than incandescent bulbs, using them can save the average household more than $200 a year in the long run. LEDs have other advantages, too. For example, they can be used in a variety of temperatures and come in lots of colors. LEDs can use **solar** power, and some can be dimmed or use sensors so that they turn on and off in certain lighting. They don't produce a lot of heat either, which makes them safer to touch.

Another type of energy-efficient light is called a **light-emitting diode (LED)**. These last 25 times longer than incandescent bulbs and use 75 percent less energy. They also last longer than CFLs.

A **diode** is a **semiconductor** that conducts an electric current, but only partly. It lets electricity flow in one direction, but if it tries to flow the other way, it can't get through. LED bulbs are more expensive to buy, but are cheaper to use in the long run because they last longer than other bulbs and help reduce strain on the power grid. And because they last longer, they reduce waste in **landfills**.

Should governments nudge people and businesses toward making decisions that keep the planet healthier?

In 1879, the Sarah Jordan Boarding House became the first house wired for electricity. You can learn more about it and tour the inside here. **What looks different about the wiring in this house from the wiring in your house?**

🔍 Sarah Jordan Boarding House, Edison

PS

What do you think? Should people have a choice to buy either incandescent or more energy-efficient light bulbs?

ELECTRICITY

> **WORDS TO KNOW**
>
> **direct current (DC):** an electric current where electricity flows in one direction.
>
> **alternating current (AC):** an electric current where electricity flows back and forth.
>
> **power plant:** a place where electric power is produced to be spread out and used.

AC AND DC

Electricity can travel in different ways. **Direct current (DC)** moves in only one direction in a circuit. Batteries produce direct current. We use DC in devices such as cellphones, flashlights, and laptop computers when they aren't plugged in. The electricity flows from the positive end of the battery to the negative end through a conductor until we turn off the device with a switch.

In an **alternating current (AC)** electrons vibrate back and forth and change direction in a circuit. When electricity must travel across long distances, AC is used more often than DC. Most electric power coming from wall outlets in our homes and schools is alternating current. This is because AC is less expensive to use, easier to change the voltage along the way (or keep it steady), and loses less energy during the transmission.

The Centennial Light Bulb

The average lifespan of an incandescent bulb is between 750 and 2,000 hours. But there's one that's lasted for more than a million hours! The Centennial Light Bulb hangs from the ceiling in a fire station in Livermore, California. It was made by the Shelby Electric Company and was first put in use in 1901. It's been off a few times to be moved and during a power shortage, but it still works. It's a 60W bulb and currently shines at about 4W.

To learn more and see this record-breaking bulb, visit this website.

Centennial Light Bulb

46

CIRCUITS

THE WAR OF THE CURRENTS

Nikola Tesla (1856–1943) was a great scientist with many ideas about electricity. He worked for Thomas Edison. The two of them got in a big argument about the best kind of current for sending out electricity. Their battle became known as "The War of Currents."

Edison thought DC was better and safer because you could keep the voltage lower. He might have also thought it was better because he had many patents for the DC system, which meant he'd make lots of money! And Tesla thought AC was better because you could easily change the voltage and it could go longer distances. Tesla didn't invent AC, but he had improved it.

The United States has three power grids: East, West, and Texas. In February 2021, Texas experienced a stretch of extreme cold and its power grid went down. This led to hundreds of deaths and resulted in more than $300 billion in damage.

It turns out they were both right. Today, we use AC to bring electricity into our homes and buildings via **power plants**. For some things, such as light bulbs, it doesn't matter which kind is used, AC or DC. But things with more complicated electrical systems need DC.

47

ELECTRICITY

WORDS TO KNOW

rectifier: a device that converts AC electricity into DC.

substation: a special power plant where electricity is reduced in voltage so it can be used in homes, offices, and so on.

transformer: a device that changes the voltage of an alternating current.

breaker panel: the electric box that distributes the electricity coming into a house or other building to each outlet and switch.

To see how power companies send electricity to our homes, check out this video. **How do all the different parts of the power grid work together?**

🔎 SDGE electricity home

So, AC electricity is converted into DC using a device called a **rectifier**. Some examples of things that convert AC into DC include computers, televisions, and appliances. Today, we use both AC and DC in our homes, buildings, appliances, and electronics.

HOW DOES ELECTRICITY MAKE IT TO OUR HOMES?

It's easy to flick a switch and be aware of the electricity that lights up the room. But where did that electricity come from? How did it get inside your house? And is there a chance it will run out?

To supply large areas with electricity, we use a system of power plants called a power grid. You can think of this grid as one giant circuit. These grids connect to other grids across the country and sometimes even across continents. The power plant closest to you is likely connected to a power plant on the other side of the country!

How does the power grid work? First, power plants produce electricity using different methods. We'll learn about these methods in later chapters. Next, the electricity is sent out along power lines to smaller power plants, called **substations**.

CIRCUITS

From the substations, the electricity goes into **transformers**. A transformer is a device that either raises or lowers the voltage of the electricity. Raising the voltage helps push the electricity along the grid—that's how the electricity keeps traveling from transformer to transformer. Finally, the electricity reaches a transformer that lowers it to a voltage that is safe to use at home.

Air Force One, **the plane that flies the president of the United States, has around 240 miles of electric wires in it!**

The electricity goes into your house through a meter, which measures how much electricity is being used. The electricity then flows to a circuit **breaker panel**—the main distribution point for electric circuits in your house. It's very much like a switchboard for your house, telling the electricity where to go. If you look inside (ask an adult to do this with you), you'll see multiple switch boxes. Each of these switches directs electricity to different places. For example, you may see one for a large appliance such as a clothes dryer or one for a whole room.

A Brief History of Power Grids

After the War of the Currents, businesspeople began building commercial AC power plants. Soon, there were lots companies trying to win over costumers. Since more people lived in cities, that's where the power plants were built, which meant people who didn't live near a city were out of luck. The other problem was that there were no rules. So, safety could be issue.

Following the end of the Great Depression in 1933, the U.S. government decided electric companies needed to have rules. It also decided that electricity should be available to everyone, not just the rich or those in cities. By the mid-1960s, power grids were formed. A power grid is a network of power plants and their systems that are working together.

Today, the United States has three power grids. There's one that covers the East and one that covers the West. The third one covers Texas. This last one is called the ERCOT grid.

ELECTRICITY

The breakers are used for safety. If one detects a problem in its circuit, it automatically shuts the flow of electricity. When this happens, you can usually just safely switch them back on. You can use the breaker box to turn off all the electricity coming into your house if there's an emergency, such as a flood. From the breaker panel, electric wires run throughout your house, into outlets, and into electric devices.

As we've learned, electricity follows a path. It flows through a circuit and can be moved across great distances using power plants, right into our homes and businesses. Ideally, when you need to turn on something, electricity is there. But did you know that wherever you find electricity, you'll also find something else? Magnetism! Let's take a look in the next chapter.

Career Corner

If you're interested in working with electricity, there are lots of jobs you could do. Here are just a few.

- **Electricians** work in homes and businesses installing and repairing electric lines, circuit breakers, and other systems, and make sure they all meet the electric codes, or rules.

- **Line workers** install, maintain, and repair electric wires that are overhead or below ground.

- **Power grid engineers or operators** design, fix, and maintain electric power grids or run a power plant.

- **Electrical engineers** research or develop electric equipment, fix or anticipate future problems, and test new things.

- **Renewable energy technicians or power system engineers** keep alternative energy systems such as solar or wind up and running and connected to other sources of power.

- **Automotive electricians** install and fix the electric components in cars when something goes wrong.

ESSENTIAL QUESTION

How does electricity travel across the country and into our homes and businesses?

SIMPLE CLOSED CIRCUIT

> **TOOL KIT**
> ° aluminum foil
> ° electric tape
> ° 2 D batteries
> ° light bulb from a flashlight
> ° wooden clothespin
> ° science journal

When you did the Voltaic Pile project in Chapter 2, you made an open circuit. Now, let's make a simple closed circuit.

❯ **Cut two pieces of aluminum foil, each about 12 by 2 inches.** Fold and pinch each into a long, skinny, ribbon-like strip. Use electric tape to fasten one end of one of the aluminum strips to the positive end of one battery.

❯ **Tape one end of the second aluminum strip to the negative end of the same battery.** Tape the other end of this aluminum strip to the ring of metal at the bottom of the light bulb.

❯ **Pinch open the clothespin and carefully slide the bulb inside.** This will make the bulb easier to hold when you do the next step.

❯ **The bottom of the light bulb should have a tiny metal base.** Holding the bulb in the clothespin, touch the loose end of the first aluminum strip to the base of the light bulb. Make sure the two pieces of aluminum strips aren't touching each other.

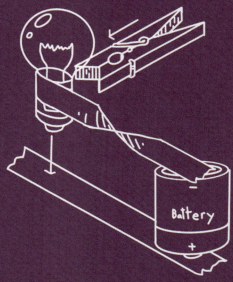

❯ **What happens to the light bulb?** Does it glow? Is it dim or bright? Write what you observe in your journal. What do you think will happen if you add the second battery to the circuit? Write down your prediction.

❯ **Tape the second battery to the first one, making sure the positive end of the first battery touches the negative end of the second battery.** Tape the piece of aluminum that was on the negative end of the first battery to the negative end of the second battery. What happens? Why do you think that's happening? Write down your ideas and observations in your journal.

Try This!

Aluminum foil is a conductor. What are some other things around your home that are made of aluminum? Does this mean they are all conductors, too? Can you think of a way to test your theory?

51

FLASHLIGHT

Using what you've learned about circuits and some household items, you can make your own flashlight!

> **Caution:** You will need an adult to help you with the drill, utility knife, and hot glue gun

> **TOOL KIT**
> ° 2 C batteries
> ° electrical tape
> ° 2 medicine bottles (1¼-inch diameter) with safety caps
> ° drill
> ° utility knife
> ° 10-mm LED light (rated 3 volts)
> ° hot glue gun
> ° scissors
> ° aluminum foil
> ° cardboard
> ° ribbon or string

❯ **Tape the two batteries together end-to-end with electric tape.** You are making one long battery with a positive end and a negative end. Set your long battery aside for now.

❯ **Remove and recycle one of the medicine bottle caps.** Have an adult drill a hole in the middle of the second cap. It's easier to do if you leave the lid on the bottle. The hole should be big enough for the LED to fit inside snuggly. This will be your flashlight's reflector.

❯ **Ask an adult to use the utility knife to cut off the bottoms of the bottles.** If you're using bottles that are 2½ inches long, cut off about ¼ inch from each. Tape the bottles together to create a long tube.

❯ **Slid the long battery inside the tube until it touches the bottom of the cap.** The negative end of the battery should be about half an inch from the end of the tube. If it is not, you may have to cut one of the bottles shorter. After you've checked, remove the battery.

❯ **Set the LED inside the hole you drilled, with the leads hanging down.** Ask an adult to help you use hot glue to keep the bulb in place.

❯ **When the glue is dry, bend the positive lead 90 degrees and then twist it into a half-circle.** Bend the negative lead 90 degrees in the opposite direction.

TEXT TO WORLD

How did competition between Tesla and Edison result in a better power grid for today's users?

❯ **Cut a piece of foil that's 6 inches by 2 inches.** Roll and press it into a flat ribbon that's about half an inch wide. Tape one end of the foil ribbon to the negative lead of the LED. Make sure the two are tightly connected.

❯ **Carefully bend the foil so it'll slide along the inside of the tube.** Screw the cap back on, still upside-down. Slide the battery back inside the tube so that the negative end is touching the bottom of the cap.

❯ **Bend the extra bit of foil at the bottom so it touches the negative end of the battery inside the tube.** The LED should light up when you press on the foil.

❯ **To make an off/on button, cut a piece of cardboard 4 inches by ½ inch.** Crease it so it looks like a flat-bottom "U." Tie a piece of ribbon or string around the bottom. You can tape it in place if you'd like.

❯ **Slide the cardboard inside the tube and alongside the battery.** When you want to turn on the flashlight, push the cardboard inside the tube until it causes the foil to connect to the negative end of the battery. To turn off your flashlight, pull the string until the cardboard stops pressing on the foil.

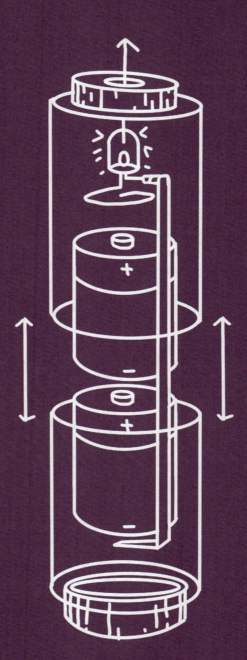

Try This!

Use electric tape or duct tape in multiple colors to decorate the outside of your flashlight.

PAPER CLIP SWITCH

> **TOOL KIT**
> ◦ simple, closed circuit
> ◦ large paper clip
> ◦ cardboard
> ◦ 2 pushpins
> ◦ science journal

Switches allow you to control the flow of electricity. Here's an easy way to add one to your simple circuit.

▶ **Cut through one of the foil strips from your simple circuit, halfway between the battery and the bulb.** Open the paper clip, leaving a loop at each end. You should now have two pieces of foil about 6 inches long.

▶ **Place one end of the cut foil strip on the cardboard.** Stick a pushpin through one loop of the paper clip, through the foil, and into the cardboard. Some of the metal should be showing and the paper clip should be able to move.

▶ **Using the other pushpin, attach the other foil strip to the other end of the cardboard.** It should be close enough so that the paper clip reaches the other pushpin. The paper clip should be able to swing between the two pushpins.

▶ **Try your switch!** Swing the paper clip to touch the metal part of the second pushpin. Is your light glowing? If not, make sure the foil strips haven't come loose from the light or battery.

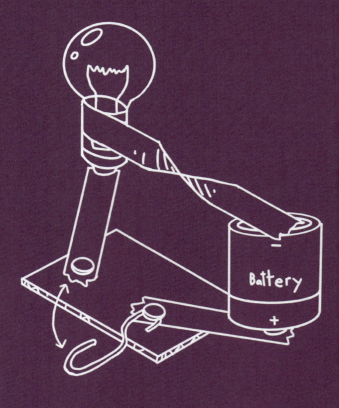

Try This!

Can you think of other materials that might work instead of a paper clip? Use a scientific method worksheet to organize your experiment. Then try the materials and see if they work.

Chapter 4

ELECTROMAGNETISM

You might not think magnets and electricity are related. After all, they do different things! But magnets and electricity have many similarities. And they happen to be very closely connected.

It's fun to play with magnets. You can make them pick up things or stick to certain objects. And if you put two magnets close together, sometimes they stick to each other and sometimes they push away, or repel, each other, depending on their positions. Sounds a lot like objects with an electric charge, right?

Magnetism is a force that either attracts or repels materials that are like it. Electricity and magnetism are connected. Where you find one, you will always find the other.

> **ESSENTIAL QUESTION**
>
> How is electromagnetism related to electricity?

55

ELECTRICITY

WORDS TO KNOW

magnetism: a force caused by the motion of electrons that either attracts objects or repels them.

compass: an instrument that uses a magnetized needle to find north.

magnetic field: the invisible area around a magnet that pulls objects to it or pushes them away.

One of the first people to discover this connection was Hans Christian Oersted (1777–1851). Oersted was a college professor from Denmark. One day, he was talking to his students about electricity when he accidentally passed a wire with an electric current over a **compass**. When he did, the compass needle changed direction.

Instead of pointing north, the needle pointed to the wire. It was following the flow of the electric current. This showed Oersted that the electricity in the wire had magnetism.

ELECTROMAGNETISM

MAGNETIC FIELDS

Just as batteries have two different ends, a magnet has two different ends. We say a battery has a positive and negative end. With a magnet, we say it has a north pole and a south pole. And just as with charged atoms, like poles repel each other and opposite poles attract.

An invisible force flows in the space around the magnet. It goes from the north pole to the south pole and back again. This force doesn't just go everywhere. It stays in a certain area called a **magnetic field**.

> How do scientists know what the magnetic field around a planet looks like? They use some very sensitive equipment. **Learn more in this video! Why might it be important to know about magnetic fields around other planets?**
>
> 🔍 NatGeo magnetic field lab
>
>

You can see the magnetic field pattern in these metal shavings.

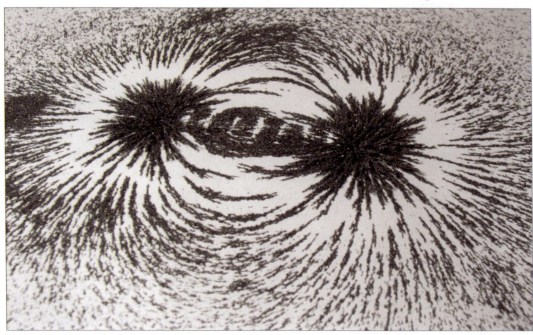

57

ELECTRICITY

WORDS TO KNOW

wave: a curving movement in water, air, ground, or other object.

electromagnet: a type of magnet where the magnetic field is produced by electricity.

Michael Faraday is often called the "Father of Electricity." Along with showing that a moving magnetic field can create electricity, he discovered that electric charges put out "waves." We use these waves to send sounds across the radio.

Any object with magnetism has a magnetic field. The magnetic field is strongest right around the object. It gets weaker farther away from the object. You'll know your magnet is inside another magnet's magnetic field when you feel a push or pull.

Oersted's discovery that an electric current creates a magnetic field was important. A few years later, a British scientist named Michael Faraday (1791–1867) showed that a moving magnetic field creates an electric current. He pushed a magnetic rod back and forth through a bundle of wire. When the rod wasn't moving, there wasn't a charge. But when the rod was moving, there was an electric charge. The magnetic field was moving the electrons in the wire. And electrons in motion mean one thing—electricity.

Michael Faraday

Michael Faraday was born in what is now a part of South London, England. His family was poor and Faraday received only a basic education. But when he was a young teenager, he began working for a bookbinder. He read a lot of books! And he became interested in science and did experiments at night. When he was in his early 20s, Faraday began working for Sir Humphry Davy (1778–1829), a famous chemist. Davy took Faraday around the world, and this allowed Faraday to learn even more from other scientists. Later, Faraday began studying electricity.

Faraday's work with electromagnetism led to the first electric motor and generator. We'll learn more about motors and generator in Chapter 5. His work in chemistry was also important. Among other things, he discovered benzene, a chemical used in many things such as paint, synthetic fibers, and glues. He also did experiments in how to liquefy gases, which eventually led to the invention of refrigerators.

58

ELECTROMAGNETISM

A Scottish physicist named James Clerk Maxwell (1831–1879) combined the discoveries of Oersted, Faraday, and others into one theory called electromagnetism. This theory states that electricity and magnetism are two parts of the same force. Electromagnetism is the magnetic force created by a current of electricity.

SUPER MAGNETS: ELECTROMAGNETS

The magnets you use to stick things on your refrigerator or to pick up small metal objects are called permanent magnets. They keep their magnetism all the time. But by using electricity, we can make magnets that turn on and off. These magnets are called **electromagnets**.

Electromagnets are made by first wrapping an insulated wire around an iron rod. Then, an electric current is sent through the wire. What happens? A magnetic field forms around the iron rod, and the rod becomes magnetic. Once the current is turned off, the rod stops being magnetic.

Why might this be useful? Electromagnets are all around you in things you use every day, such as car locks, doorbells, telephones, and refrigerators.

This electromagnet is dropping metal junk onto a junk pile.

59

ELECTRICITY

We can also control the power of an electromagnet. A huge iron rod with a lot of wire wrapped around it makes a strong magnet! The more wire, the stronger the magnetism. Junkyards use large electromagnets to lift and move heavy objects such as cars and scrap metal. Some roller coasters use them to hold and stop cars along the track.

Learn more about electromagnetism in this video. **How does the number of wires affect the power of the magnet?**

Science Buddies electromagnets

There are many other places where electromagnets are used. One of the biggest industries that rely on them are the automotive companies that make electric and hybrid cars. The motors in these types of cars use opposing magnetic fields to turn a car's axle, the rod that rotates the wheels.

Another place where electromagnets are widely used is in robotics. The medical field also uses them. For example, you need electromagnetics for MRI machines. In fact, just about any job that works with or needs any kind of motor or generator relies on electromagnetism.

If you like electromagnets, maybe you could become a robotics engineer!

60

ELECTROMAGNETISM

EARTH HAS NORTH AND SOUTH POLES, TOO!

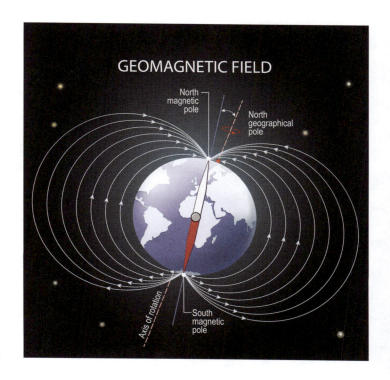

Magnets have a north and a south end. What else has a north and south end? Planet Earth! Earth is similar to a giant magnet. You can't see it, but our planet has a magnetic field all around it. The northernmost point of this magnetic field is the North Pole. The southernmost point of the magnetic field is the South Pole. The poles do not stay in one place. They move around a little bit each day.

A compass will always point toward the North Pole. This can be useful if you're lost. If you can find north, you can find other directions, too.

Roller Coaster Magnetism

Magnets are used in all kinds of machines. They are even used in roller coasters. Very strong magnets along the track repel a metallic fin that's on the bottom or side of the roller coaster train. This in turn can launch cars up to speeds of 100 miles per hour in just seconds.

Magnets are used to slow down or stop roller coasters, too. The first roller coaster to use a magnetic braking system was the *Millennium Force* at Cedar Point in Sandusky, Ohio. It was built in 2000. Today, many roller coasters use magnets to brake because they don't need replacing very often and they save electricity.

61

ELECTRICITY

> Maglev trains (short for magnetic levitation trains) use strong magnetic fields to hover over the tracks. Because the trains aren't touching anything, there's no rolling resistance so they can travel at incredible speeds. Watch a maglev train in action in this video. **What do you notice about the way it moves?**
>
> 🔍 Lesics maglev

Compasses use a needle that has been magnetized. The needle can spin freely. One end is usually marked in red or with an "N." Because the needle is magnetized, it lines up with Earth's magnetic field. The needle shows which direction is north.

Magnetic vs. Geographic Poles

Think of the earth as a ball with a long pole going right through the middle of it, from top to bottom. At one end of this pole would be the geographic North Pole. At the other end of this pole would be the geographic South Pole. The geographic poles don't move. But the magnetic poles (the most northern and southern points of the earth's magnetic field) do move around a little each day. This is because magnetic fields change slightly as things rotate.

Even though the geographic poles don't change, if you planted flags at those points, the flags would move a little each day. This is because the ice in which you planted your flags is moving!

As we've explored in this chapter, magnets and electricity go hand in hand. You can't have one without the other. And now that we've learned what electromagnetism is, let's explore what goes hand in hand with it. (Spoiler alert: It's motors and generators!)

ESSENTIAL QUESTION

How is electromagnetism related to electricity?

MAGNETIC
FIELD VIEWER

You can see magnetic fields in action with one of these easy-to-make viewers.

▶ **Fill your bottle with the mineral oil until the oil is about 1 inch to 1½ inches from the lid.**

▶ **Use the funnel to carefully add 2 tablespoons of iron filings to the oil.** Depending on the size of your bottle, you can add more or fewer iron filings. When you're done, screw the lid tightly on the bottle.

▶ **Shake the bottle so the iron filings mix with the oil.** What do you think will happen if you place the magnet near the bottle? Write down your prediction in your science journal.

▶ **Lay the magnet on a flat surface.** Place your viewer just above the magnet. (It's okay if the magnet attaches itself to the bottle.) What happens? You should be able to see the magnetic field of the magnet. Can you see the magnet's poles? Draw what you see in your science journal.

TOOL KIT
- clean glass or plastic salad dressing bottle (or similar flat bottle) with lid
- mineral oil (found at most drug or grocery stores)
- funnel
- iron filings
- bar magnet
- science journal

Try This!

What do you think would happen to the iron filings if you moved the magnet around or used a magnet of a different shape? Experiment and find out!

Magnet Warnings

Never put a magnet in your mouth. (And keep them away from your younger brothers and sisters, too.) Magnets can hurt you if you swallow them. This is because if you swallow two or more magnets, they can become stuck together inside your body and squeeze together things such as your intestines and make you sick. Even a single magnet can be dangerous because it could cause you to choke or become lodged in your lungs. Be careful when experimenting with magnets!

MAKE A COMPASS

TOOL KIT
- glass dish
- water
- plastic lid from a milk jug
- sewing needle

Compasses were invented in ancient China. They were first used as part of fortune telling. It wasn't until much later that people saw how useful a compass could be to help them find their way around. You can't take this compass on a hike, but you can use it at home.

▶ **Fill the dish with about 2 inches of water.** Place the lid in the water. It doesn't matter if it's face up or down, as long as it's floating.

▶ **Moving from the eye of the needle to the sharp pointy end, run the magnet along the needle.** Go in only one direction. (Don't rub it back and forth, or it won't work.) Rub the needle about 20 times to magnetize the needle.

▶ **Carefully lay the needle on top of the floating lid.** What happens? The tip of the needle should slowly move to point north.

Try This!

Instead of laying your needle on a lid, try (carefully) pushing it through a cork or laying it on top of a piece of wax paper.

Compass Rose

A compass rose is a symbol found on maps, charts, and even the ground at many airports. Some resemble stars, while others look like wheels. They are used to help us identify **magnetic north**.

The world's largest compass rose is in a dry lakebed in the Mojave Desert in California. The **diameter** of this compass rose is more than 4,000 feet! It helps airplanes landing at Edwards Air Force Base **calibrate** their aircraft's magnetic compass.

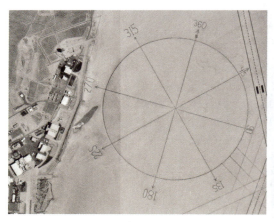
Credit: NASA

WORDS TO KNOW

magnetic north: the direction the north end of a compass will point in response to Earth's magnetic field.

diameter: the straight line that goes from one side of a circle, through its center, to the other side.

calibrate: to fix an instrument to a standard reading.

ELECTROMAGNET

For this project, you will need a screwdriver that is not magnetized. To test whether the screwdriver is magnetized, try picking up a paper clip or nail with the tip of the screwdriver before you begin.

TOOL KIT
- non-magnetized screwdriver
- insulted wire
- electric tape
- 2 D batteries
- paper clips

CAUTION: Ask an adult to strip the wire. Also, be careful once your electromagnet is on because it will get hot. Don't forget to turn it off when you're done.

▶ **Wrap the wire tightly around the metal part of the screwdriver in a spiral.** Make as many loops around the screwdriver as you can without overlapping them. The more loops your electromagnet has, the more power it will have. Leave 2 inches of the screwdriver uncovered and leave about 5 inches of loose wire at the ends. You can use some electric tape to keep the coiled wire in place.

▶ **Ask an adult to use scissors to carefully strip off about 1 inch of insulation at each end of the wire.**

▶ **Stack the batteries with the positive end of one touching the negative end of the other.** Wrap the middle with electric tape. You should now have a long battery with a positive end and a negative end.

▶ **Tape one end of the stripped wire to the positive side of the battery.** Tape the other end of the stripped wire to the negative end of the battery.

▶ **Your electromagnet is on.** Hold the screwdriver by the handle. See if you can pick up the paper clips. Be careful! The longer you use your electromagnet, the hotter your wires and battery will become.

Try This!

How many paper clips do you think your electromagnet can pick up? Make a prediction and test it. Do you think you could pick up something bigger than a paper clip?

TEXT TO WORLD

Can you find a device that uses an electromagnet in your house? How do you know? Can you think of ways to make that device more efficient?

65

MAGNETIC
SLIME

Magnetic slime and a magnet—what could be more fun?

> **TOOL KIT**
> - 1 cup white glue
> - ¼ cup liquid starch
> - ½ cup water
> - bowl
> - cookie sheet
> - iron filings
> - a variety of magnets

Note: This slime is only good for one day since the iron filings rust quickly and change the consistency of the slime.

❯ **Pour the glue, liquid starch, and water into the bowl.** Use a spoon to stir the ingredients together.

❯ **Use your hands to knead the slime.** You want it to be smooth and stretchy.

❯ **Spread the slime into a small circle on the cookie sheet.** Sprinkle iron filings onto the slime. The more iron filings you add, the more magnetic your slime will be.

❯ **Knead the iron filings into the slime.** You want them to be fully incorporated.

❯ **Ready to have some fun?** Use a variety of magnets to get the slime to move or jump or place a magnet in the middle of the slime and watch what happens.

Try This!

Slime is considered a non-Newtonian fluid, which is neither a solid nor a liquid. You can pick it up (like a solid) but it will ooze and change shape to fill a container (like a liquid).

Make another non-Newtonian fluid. Pour a box of cornstarch into a bowl. Slowly add water and stir, using your hands if you'd like, until the mixture becomes tough to stir, like a thick syrup. Quickly poke the top of the mixture. Does it resist? Next, slowly poke the mixture. How does it behave now? What happens if you squish the mixture in your hand?

Chapter 5

MOTORS AND
GENERATORS

What do fans, refrigerators, electric pencil sharpeners, and remote-control toys have in common? They all have motors. Electric motors are machines that change electric power into motion. This kind of motion, like the spinning blades of a fan, is called **mechanical** power. And guess what? All electric motors, big and small, use magnets to create that mechanical power.

ESSENTIAL QUESTION

How do motors and generators use magnets?

If you took apart an electric motor, you'd see magnets inside. Some are permanent magnets, and some are electromagnets. A small motor has two permanent magnets with the opposite poles facing each other. Between those poles is something invisible but strong—a magnetic field.

67

ELECTRICITY

WORDS TO KNOW

mechanical: related to machines or tools.

armature: the spinning part of a motor, made of tightly coiled wires.

axle: a rod on which something spins.

winding: wire wrapped around an armature.

commutator: the part of a motor that reverses the electric current.

brush: a soft, springy, metal wire that, with a commutator, acts as a switch inside a motor.

GO, MOTOR, GO!

Let's look at how motors work. The spinning part of the motor is an electromagnet called the **armature**. The armature sits inside the magnetic field and is made of a wire coiled tightly around a metal **axle**. An axle is a rod that spins, or rolls. It's what turns the tires on a bike, makes the wheels turn on a remote-control car, and spins the blades that sharpen a pencil. An axle makes objects move.

On its own, the armature does nothing. But when an electric current passes through the **windings** of the coil, the axle becomes a magnet. It has a north pole and a south pole. But how does this create motion?

The coil turns to find its opposite charge on the permanent magnet—remember, opposite poles attract and like poles repel. But we don't want the spinning to just stop there. That wouldn't produce much motion.

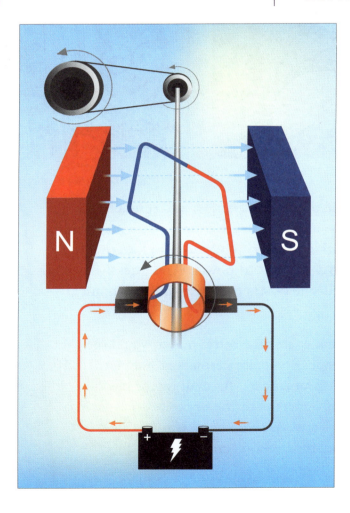

68

MOTORS AND GENERATORS

To keep the electric current flowing, it needs to be changing direction. On a permanent magnet, the poles are always in the same place. But on an electromagnet, we can flip-flop the poles by changing the flow of the electric current. The magnet must keep spinning to find its opposite pole. That's what keeps an electric motor moving.

How many things in your home use a motor? How would your life be different without electric motors?

You probably know people who commute to work. They must travel back and forth to get to their place of business. A DC electric motor has something called a **commutator** that makes the electric current travel back and forth. Some AC motors, such as repulsion or universal motors, use commutators, too. It's like a metal ring split in half. Each half wraps around the part of the axle that sticks out the end of the armature.

Both sides of the commutator have a soft, springy, metal wire attached, called a **brush**. Each brush attaches to a positive or negative end of a power source, such as a battery.

You might find this small motor in appliances in your home!

69

ELECTRICITY

WORDS TO KNOW

mechanical energy: energy that uses physical parts you can see, such as the parts of a machine. It is related to motion and height.

transistor: a device that controls the flow of electricity.

turbine: a device that uses pressure on blades to spin generators and create electricity.

Motors, by definition, turn one type of energy into mechanical energy, motion. But not all motors use electricity. For example, diesel engines and locomotive engines use heat to create motion.

Together, the commutator and brushes act as a switch. Their job is to keep shifting the magnetic field so the armature continues to spin.

In a simple motor, the permanent magnets are stationary and the electromagnet spins. In motors without brushes or a commutator, the permanent magnet is inside the magnetic field of the electromagnets instead of the other way around. The trick is to change the direction of the electric current on the electromagnets at the right time to keep the permanent magnet spinning.

Turn Up the Heat!

Can you imagine traveling in a car in the winter without heat? *Brrr!* Thanks to mechanical engineer Margaret A. Wilcox (1838–unknown), vehicles now have heat to keep both humans and cargo warm. Car heaters weren't Wilcox's first invention, but because of the laws in the 1800s, women weren't allowed to file patents under their own names, so her inventions were credited to her husband. But by 1893, Wilcox received a patent under her own name for the system she invented that ran a channel of air through the hot engine and back out into the vehicle cabin, making it much warmer for the occupants. Of course, most cars and trucks weren't closed in yet, so it was another few decades before engineers, using Wilcox's design, figured out how to regulate the temperature for passengers.

MOTORS AND GENERATORS

This is done with a computer and a **transistor,** which controls the flow of electricity. It's like a faucet that controls how much and how fast water comes out a tap.

GENERATORS

An electric current can create a magnetic field. And a magnetic field can create an electric current. We see something similar happening with motors. A motor uses electricity to create mechanical force, but we can reverse the action.

The Hoover Dam on the border of Arizona and Nevada uses water from the Colorado River to push **turbines**. These turbines power 17 huge generators that create enough electricity for more than a million people. Take a virtual tour of the dam with this video. **What happens to the water turbines as the water level in the dam decreases?**

What's Inside Hoover Dam

We can use mechanical force (or motion) to turn the motor and create electricity. The machine that does this is called a generator.

These wind turbines are moved by the air that blows on them.

ELECTRICITY

WORDS TO KNOW

momentum: a force that keeps an object moving after it has begun to move.

radio wave: a type of invisible wave used to transmit radio and television signals. Radio waves are also used for navigation.

Tesla coil: a device used for research that can produce high-voltage electricity.

Electric generators work in an opposite way than electric motors. They produce electricity when their rotating part is turned by an engine. Generators can be useful to have on hand when your power goes out!

How does a generator turn the armature to make electricity? Does somebody have to stand there and spin it by hand? No! That method would take a lot of work to create enough electricity for a whole house or city! A generator includes a turbine. It's like a wheel with wide blades. Pressure from water, steam, or air spins the blades.

You've probably played on a swing. Sometimes, you need an extra push at the beginning to get moving. Then, you can pump yourself to keep moving and maintain your **momentum**.

If a motor has a big job to do, such as getting a furnace going or a washing machine spinning, it needs a push to get started. This extra push of electricity comes from a capacitor, which stores an electric charge until it's needed. Capacitors are used in almost every type of electronic gadget, from small laptops and digital cameras to big hybrid cars and MRI machines.

OKAY, JUST ONE LAST ADJUSTMENT . . .

HOW DOES THAT FEEL? IS IT WORKING NOW?

PERFECT! IT'S WORKING BETTER THAN EVER!

MOTORS AND GENERATORS

A Tesla coil

TESLA KEEPS INVENTING

In Chapter 3 we learned how Nikola Tesla had a big falling out with Thomas Edison over which type of current was best for distributing electricity: AC or DC. After Tesla stopped working with Edison, he began his own experiments. One of his most useful inventions was a motor without brushes or a commutator. Brushes can wear out quickly and motors without commutators run more smoothly.

Tesla also discovered **radio waves**, developed fluorescent lighting, and helped build a power plant using the force of water from Niagara Falls.

In addition, Tesla invented what's called the **Tesla coil**. This large machine can produce electricity above 1,000,000 volts! It can make sparks 130 feet long and generate 300,000 watts! Today, scientists use Tesla coils to do research and to show off the power of electricity

Have you heard of the automotive and energy company called Tesla Inc.? It was named in honor of Nikola Tesla.

ELECTRICITY

WORDS TO KNOW

collaboration: working with others.

horsepower: a unit of power equal to 746 watts.

nanobot: a tiny robot too small to see without a microscope.

nanomotor: a microscopic motor.

ultrasonic: describes a sound too high for humans to hear.

innovation: a new invention or way of doing something.

You can learn more about the Tesla coil and how Tesla hoped to use it for wireless power in this video. How did Tesla's experiences show the value of **collaboration**? The potential pitfalls of collaboration? **What are some of your experiences with collaboration?**

🔍 Tesla Coil Simple History

Horsepower

Engines are a certain kind of motor. They burn a fuel such as gas or coal to make an object move. Others uses different forms of energy, such as electricity. Have you ever heard someone say an engine has good **horsepower** and wondered what that meant?

During the late 1700s, a Scottish inventor named James Watt (1736–1819) made an improved steam engine. Engines were new and most people didn't understand what they could do. To convince people to use his engine, Watt decided to compare the engine to something people already knew about—horses. Watt observed horses pulling coal out of a mine and doing other work. He used his data to calculate a rate at which a horse could do work per minute. Then, he used this to describe his engine. For example, an engine could do the same work as one horse or two horses and so on. Horsepower quickly became a popular way to describe an engine's power. It's still used today when describing car engines! In terms of electricity, one horsepower is equal to 746 watts. Can you think of other things that are measured in terms that might not make sense at first glance?

74

MOTORS AND GENERATORS

NANOBOTS

The smallest motors are found in **nanobots**. Nanobots are super-tiny robots that scientists are working to develop. Nanobots are run by **nanomotors**. These motors are 500 times smaller than a grain of salt and run on just a single atom!

Scientists have already been able to put these motors inside live human cells and move and steer them around. This is done using **ultrasonic** waves and magnetics. In the future, scientists hope nanobots and their nanomotors can be used in medicine. For example, they might be able to travel inside the human body and locate and destroy cancer cells.

A Japanese company has built a capacitor so small that even the engineers can barely see it. It's as tiny as the period at the end of this sentence.

Take a look at this overview of motors at work. **What is similar about all the motors in your household? What are some differences between motors?**

 Owens electric motor video

Speaking of the future . . . scientists and engineers are on the lookout for ways to make electricity production more earth friendly and better for the climate. In the next chapter, we'll learn about some of the **innovations** people around the world are coming up with!

ESSENTIAL QUESTION

How do motors and generators use magnets?

WATER
TURBINE

Water turbines, such as those at the Hoover Dam, use the flow of water to generate electricity. You can build your own water turbine with just a few materials.

TOOL KIT
- utility knife
- 2-liter plastic bottle
- scissors
- metal skewer
- piece of straight cork (recycled from a bottle or from a craft store)
- science journal

Note: Ask an adult to help you use the utility knife and to push the skewer through the cork.

❯ **Ask an adult to use the utility knife to cut the plastic bottle into three, roughly equal parts.** Recycle the top of the bottle and the cap.

❯ **With the scissors, cut the middle part of the bottle into eight rectangles that are 1½ by 2½ inches.** These will be your turbine's blades.

❯ **Push the skewer lengthwise through the cork.**

❯ **Use the utility knife to cut eight equally spaced slits in the sides of the cork.** Slide a plastic blade into each slit. Make sure the curves of all the blades are facing in the same direction.

❯ **Cut a V into the side of the bottom of the bottle.** This will allow excess water to escape your turbine.

Career Connections

There are many jobs that work with electric motors. Maybe you'd like to be an electric motor mechanic or technician someday. These people work on all kinds of motors, especially those found in cars and trucks, all-electric vehicles, or hybrids, which are cars that use both electricity and gasoline to run. You can learn this job by becoming an apprentice (someone who works with an expert to learn a field), going to trade school, or completing another professional certification program.

❯ **At the top of one side of the bottom part of the bottle, cut a notch 1 inch long and ½ inch wide.** Cut a second notch on the opposite side of the bottle.

❯ **Rest your skewer inside the notches.** You want the blades to hang inside the middle of the bottle.

❯ **Ready to test your water turbine?** Place the turbine someplace where it's okay to get wet. Pour water directly on your blades. (You can use a large pitcher or a hose.) What happens when the water hits your blades? Write down what you observe.

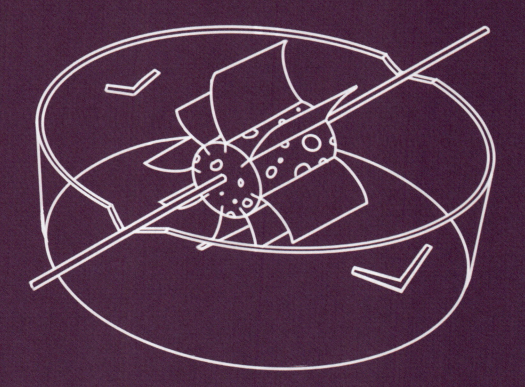

Try This!

Moving water turns the blades. Do you have a stream nearby? Set your skewer on two Y-shaped sticks in the stream. Make sure the blades are touching the water. Is the movement of water strong enough to cause the blades to spin?

77

SIMPLE
MOTOR

With a little patience, you can build your own motor!

> **TOOL KIT**
> ° magnetic copper wire
> ° D battery
> ° metal nail file
> ° 2 large paper clips
> ° plastic cup
> ° 2 ceramic magnets
> ° rubber band
> ° electric tape

❯ **Cut three pieces of wire: two that are 10 inches long and one that is 24 inches long.** Take the long piece of wire. Leaving about 3 inches of wire at the starting end, begin wrapping the wire tightly around the battery. Leave about 3 inches at the other end of the battery.

❯ **Carefully slide the coil you've made off the battery.** Tightly twist the free ends of the wire around the loop it is touching a few times. This will keep the loops together and neat. Pull the free wires out to the sides. You should have something that looks like a circle with wire arms. Flatten it as best you can. This will be your winding.

❯ **Lay the winding on a flat surface.** With the winding flat on the table, use the nail file to scrape the coating off the TOP half of the wire "arms."

❯ **Unfold the paper clips.** Straighten the bottom part but pinch the top loop closed. They should look like giant needles when you're done.

❯ **Turn the cup over.** Hold one of the magnets against the bottom of the cup with one hand. Turn the cup back over and place the second magnet inside the cup. The two magnets will attract and hold together through the cup. Place the cup upside down on a table.

❯ **Stretch the rubber band around the cup, about an inch down from the magnets.** Slide your two paper clip loops under the rubber band, one on each side of the cup. The loops of the paper clips should be sticking up above the top of the cup.

❯ **Slide your winding into the paper clip loops.** You want the winding to be close to, but not touching, the magnet. You may have to adjust the rubber band and paper clips to get it just right.

❯ **Now take the 10-inch wires.** Use the metal nail file to scrap off about an inch of the coating off each end of these wires.

❱ **Lay your battery down on the table so the positive end is on the left and the negative end is on the right.** Take one of the 10-inch wires and tape one end to the positive end of the battery. Fold the other end into a small hook.

❱ **Tape one end of the other piece of 10-inch wire to the negative end of the battery.** Fold the other end into a small hook.

❱ **To hook up your motor, wrap the positive hook to the straight end of the left side paper clip.** Wrap the negative hook to the straight end of the paper clip on the right side.

❱ **Give the winding a quick push.** It should start spinning. If it doesn't, make sure the paper clips haven't slipped out of place. But be careful, the paper clips will be warm. Also make sure the winding is balanced between the paper clips.

❱ **Be patient.** Sometimes these motors take a bit of adjusting to get them working.

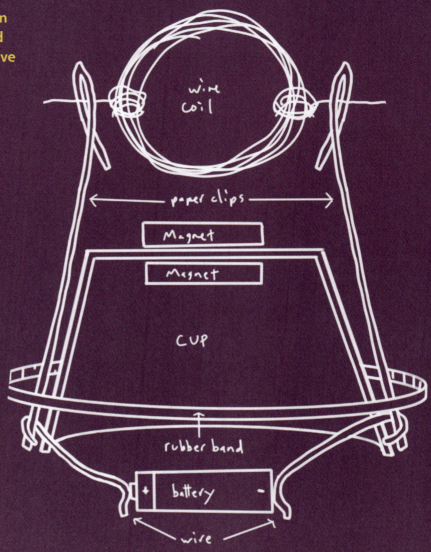

Try This!

How long can you get your motor to turn? Make a prediction and then test it out.

TEXT TO WORLD

How do you think motors and generators might change in the future?

79

ELECTROPHORUS

TOOL KIT
- aluminum pie dish
- Styrofoam cup
- masking tape
- Styrofoam plate
- wool cloth
- stopwatch
- science journal

An electrophorus is a simple capacitor. In this project you will make a capacitor and see how it works. Do this project on a cool, dry day.

❯ **Wait for a cool, dry day.** Place the pie dish face up on a table. Turn the cup over and tape it to the middle of the dish. Set this aside.

❯ **Turn the Styrofoam plate face down on a flat surface.** Gently rub the bottom of the plate with the wool cloth for 2 minutes.

❯ **Pick up the pie dish using the cup as a handle.** Set the bottom of the pie dish on top of the upside-down Styrofoam plate.

The electrophorus was invented in the 1760s by Alessandro Volta, who also invented the first cell battery. It got its name from the two Greek words elektron and phoros, which translate into "electricity bearer."

❯ **Very quickly, tap the pie dish with the tip of your finger.** What happens?

❯ **Using the cup as a handle, pick up the pie dish.** If it sticks to the Styrofoam plate, use your free hand to gently pull them apart. Hold the pie dish at least 12 inches above the Styrofoam plate.

❯ **Still holding the pie dish by the cup, quickly touch the dish with the tip of your finger again.** What happens? Did you get another zap? Why did you get zapped when you touched the aluminum pie dish? It's because the dish is holding a charge.

❯ **Predict how many times you can get a zap from the pie dish and write down your prediction in your science journal.** See if other people can touch the pie plate and get a shock, too.

Try This!

When you rubbed the Styrofoam plate, you gave it a negative charge. The aluminum pie dish was neutrally charged when you set it on top of the plate. When you touched the pie dish, you drew off some of the electrons. This gave the pie dish a positive charge.

If you used your electrophorus on a humid day, what do you think would change? Try it and find out.

Chapter 6

EARTH-FRIENDLY
ELECTRICITY

We need to take care of our planet. After all, we don't have an extra one lying around! Today, we burn enormous quantities of fossil fuels such as coal, oil, and natural gas to make electricity. Burning these fossil fuels—especially coal—creates **pollution**.

They are also **natural resources** that are **nonrenewable**. We will eventually run out of fossil fuels, and we can't make more of them. That's why scientists and engineers are working to find new ways of generating electricity that are Earth-friendly. They are also working to improve existing ways of generating electricity and trying to make devices that use electricity more efficiently, so those devices use less energy. Both things will help our planet.

ESSENTIAL QUESTION

How can we generate electricity in more Earth-friendly ways?

ELECTRICITY

WORDS TO KNOW

pollution: harmful materials that damage the air, water, and soil. These include chemicals and factory waste.

natural resource: a material such as coal, timber, water, or land that is found in nature and is useful to humans.

nonrenewable: a resource such as coal that, once used, is gone forever.

carbon dioxide: a gas formed by the burning of fossil fuels, the rotting of plants and animals, and the breathing out of animals or humans.

greenhouse gas: a gas such as water vapor, carbon dioxide, carbon monoxide, or methane that traps heat and contributes to warming temperatures.

renewable: something that isn't used up, that can be replaced.

advantage: something helpful.

disadvantage: something that causes difficulty or trouble.

solar power: energy that comes from the sun.

solar cell: a device that converts the energy of the sun into electric energy.

solar array: a collection of solar panels.

Earth is currently experiencing climate change, meaning long-term changes in weather patterns. What do you know about the climate crisis the world is facing right now? Here are just a few facts according to NASA.

• **Carbon dioxide**, a **greenhouse gas**, is up to around 417 parts per million, the highest it's ever been.

• The global temperature is up a little more than 2 degrees Fahrenheit since the 1880s, when we began keeping track. Most of this warming trend has occurred in the last 40 years.

• The years 2016 and 2020 tied as the warmest on record.

• The oceans are also warming and rising. Sea levels have gone up 8 inches in the last 100 years.

• The earth's ice is being lost. Greenland lost an average of more than 270 billion tons of ice each year in the last 30 years.

• Coal, oil, and natural gas are natural resources and are not **renewable**. A renewable resource is one that doesn't run out and that nature replaces. For example, wind is a renewable resource, as is sunshine.

Let's look at some of the renewable resources to create electricity. Each one has both **advantages** and **disadvantages**. By using a combination of the cleanest, most efficient types of energy, we can help the planet grow healthy again.

EARTH-FRIENDLY ELECTRICITY

SOLAR POWER

Solar means related to the sun. **Solar power** is energy from the sun converted to electricity. So how is solar energy collected? Usually, large panels that are made up of smaller panels called **solar cells** are placed on rooftops or in open spaces where they are exposed to sunlight.

Solar farms are areas that are dedicated to solar panels. These systems are called **solar arrays**.

The northernmost and southernmost areas of Earth experience polar nights for half the year and midnight sun for the other half. During these times, night and day last more than 24 hours because of the position of the sun. That makes solar power tricky to organize!

83

ELECTRICITY

WORDS TO KNOW

environmental impact: effect on the environment.

hydropower: energy produced by the movement of water.

medieval: the period of time in European history from about 350 CE to about 1450 CE. Also called the Middle Ages.

drought: a period of time when no precipitation falls on a region, causing problems for farms and wildlife.

When sunlight hits the top layer of these solar cells, electrons move up from the bottom layer to the top layer. The two layers are then charged differently. When the two layers are connected, electricity starts to flow. From there, the DC electricity flows into a solar inverter, which turns the electricity into AC. The AC power is then carried into homes or businesses. If there's extra electricity, it flows to the power grid or is stored in solar batteries to be used later.

Advantages: Using solar power has little **environmental impact**. It creates zero pollution. Sunlight is everywhere, and it is renewable.

Solar Power in Space

The International Space Station (ISS), a space craft orbiting the earth, has been occupied by astronauts from many countries since 2000. In space, there is no power grid. So, what does the ISS do for electricity? It uses solar energy, of course!

The ISS has eight large, foldable solar cells, called solar arrays. These solar arrays are 112 feet long and 39 feet wide. They rotate to follow the sun's light. When they're in use, they provide the ISS (and the scientists aboard) 60 percent of its electricity. When the ISS isn't in direct sunlight, it uses the electricity stored in a battery.

To see how this works, check out this video. **Why are both the solar arrays and the batteries important to the process?**

🔎 STEMonstrations solar energy NASA

84

EARTH-FRIENDLY ELECTRICITY

Disadvantages: You need many panels to make enough electricity for a house, and panels can be expensive. Plus, making those panels requires energy and materials and the process might not be efficient. Clouds, fog, snow, and even other buildings can get in the way of rays reaching panels. Solar panels and batteries (or storage banks) take up a lot of space. It's also very difficult and expensive to take the solar panels if you move.

HYDROPOWER

Hydro is the Greek word for "water." Electricity is created when water from the tide, a wave, or a current pushes on a turbine. The turbine then moves a generator. The Hoover Dam in Nevada is an example of **hydropower** in action. So is the Itaipu Dam in South America. The Itaipu Dam sits between Paraguay and Brazil and produces the most hydroelectric power of any plant in the world. The dam provides 20 percent of Brazil's energy and almost all of Paraguay's.

Advantages: Hydropower doesn't create much pollution and can easily produce large amounts of electricity.

Disadvantages: It needs a regular source of water. Dams can also destroy land and harm fish and other wildlife. Their construction can also cause problems. In China, for example, more than a million people were displaced and important land features or archeological sites were damaged or lost when the Three Gorges Dam was built between 1994 and 2012.

Watermills, a simple type of hydropower, have been used for centuries. Ancient Greeks and people in medieval times often used them to grind grain.

Droughts can also pose a problem for hydropower. The Hoover Dam has been operating way under capacity for many years because of the severe drought conditions.

ELECTRICITY

WIND POWER

Sailboats and kites use wind power, of course. But how does wind turn into electricity? You've probably seen a wind turbine in the middle of a field or maybe even next to a building. You might have spotted wind farms where engineers take advantage of a gusty region and erect many turbines together.

Wind turbines use the wind to turn blades that move a generator. Like hydropower, wind power has been around for a long time.

Get an up-close look at wind turbines and learn more about how they work in this video. **How are modern wind turbines different from old windmills?**

🔍 Nat Geo wind turbine

PS

Do the Wave!

If you've ever gone swimming in the ocean and been knocked over by a wave, you know that waves have a ton of energy! Scientists are looking into how we might be able to harness and use that energy to create electricity. This would be very useful since millions of people in the world live on or near coastlines.

One possible way this might work is to channel waves into a smaller area to push turbines. Another way might involve using wave energy converters out in deep water to turn the motions of the ocean's waves into power.

One of the biggest challenges for this type of energy is that there's no easy way to convert waves into electricity at the moment. Dealing with harsh ocean conditions, including storms, and getting the energy to where it's needed are also challenges.

EARTH-FRIENDLY ELECTRICITY

Windmills have been used since the eighth or ninth centuries to grind grains or pump water from the ground. Today, offshore wind farms set out in water and onshore wind farms set on land are used all around the world to help produce electricity.

Advantages: Wind power has little environmental impact. In areas with strong wind, it doesn't cost much to produce energy with a wind turbine compared to many other energy sources.

Disadvantages: The wind needs to blow about 14 miles per hour for wind turbines to be effective. It takes many wind turbines to create a decent amount of electricity. Also, some people don't like the way a wind farm looks. And bats, birds, and other flying creatures can get injured by the blades.

The country of Denmark currently gets half of its energy from Earth-friendly resources, including bioenergy, solar, and wind. Bioenergy is fuel made from plants and animal waste.

ELECTRICITY

WORDS TO KNOW

geothermal energy: energy from below the surface of the earth. It can heat and cool by using differences in temperature between a structure and the earth.

hot springs: water under the earth's surface that's heated by underground volcanic activity.

organic: something that is or was living, such as wood, grass, or insects.

GEOTHERMAL POWER

Geo means "earth" and *thermal* means "heat." **Geothermal energy** is power that is generated from heat made and stored underground. Earth's core is very hot—around 9,000 degrees Fahrenheit (4,982 degrees Celsius).

In some places, heat from far underground turns water into steam that travels to the surface. We can drill into these areas and pipe the steam up. Then, we can use the steam to turn turbines and generate electricity.

Heat that comes from **hot springs** can also be used. For example, because the country Iceland is home to many hot spring areas, it is able to rely on geothermal energy for much of its power needs.

Advantages: Geothermal power creates little pollution or waste. It's renewable as long as we properly take care of the reservoirs (or water wells), and it's more reliable than some other resources, such as wind or solar.

88

EARTH-FRIENDLY ELECTRICITY

A geothermal power plant

Disadvantages: Geothermal power plants must be set where the conditions are right, and not all areas are good to drill on. Geothermal also loses energy as it travels. It can result in greenhouse gases being released into the atmosphere and cause earthquakes. Plus, it's very expensive to set up.

BIOMASS POWER

Biomass power is energy created by burning **organic** matter such as wood from trees or gas from animal waste. Grass can be squeezed into bricks, similar to the pieces of charcoal you use in a barbecue grill. When biomass is burned, it can be used to heat water and create steam to turn a turbine.

ELECTRICITY

WORDS TO KNOW

nuclear: energy produced when the nucleus of an atom is split apart.

reactor core: part of the system that splits atoms to generate energy.

radioactive: a substance made of atoms that gives off nuclear energy.

Advantages: Biomass is a renewable resource and is an inexpensive way to create electricity in poorer parts of the world. It's also easy to make.

Disadvantages: Biomass is a source of pollution because it releases carbon as it burns. Plus, biomass doesn't produce much electricity. It is mostly used to heat homes.

NUCLEAR POWER

Like many power plants, **nuclear** power plants use steam to power a generator. The centers of atoms are split inside a container called a **reactor core**. This causes the atoms to release energy that heats up water and makes steam to spin the turbines.

Advantages: Nuclear power plants easily produce large amounts of electricity. They do not generate any air pollution.

Disadvantages: An accident at a nuclear power plant can release dangerous, **radioactive** material into the air and ground. This can kill plants, animals, and people. However, far more

The National Aeronautics and Space Administration (NASA) uses nuclear energy to power the Mars Rover *Curiosity*. A rover is a mobile robot used to explore planets.

people have died from climate change than nuclear accidents. And so many people are reconsidering this form of power. For example, Bill Gates, one of the founders of the software company Microsoft, started a company called TerraPower. This company has created a new way of cooling reactors using liquid sodium to make them much safer in the event of an emergency.

EARTH-FRIENDLY ELECTRICITY

As you can see, there are many ways to create electricity that is more Earth-friendly than traditional ways. Each have their advantages and disadvantages. Which ones do you think would work best where you live?

Use this map to see where in the world renewable energy is being used. **How does your country compare to the rest of the world?**

🔎 Nat Geo mapmaker

ELECTRIFYING CAREERS

Throughout this book, you've read about some cool careers that focus on electrical work. Electricity is important in our modern world, and it'll be important to us in the future as well. In addition to the jobs we've already discovered, here are more ways people are working with electricity to improve the world.

- Simulate and model the human brain and nervous system. These parts of the human body work similarly to electricity.

- Develop power systems for robotics that work without heavy batteries—such as the ones used for the Mars rover.

Electrify Everything!

Many countries are working on developing new technologies and phasing out the old ones. Everywhere you look, all kinds of modes of transportation are now using electricity to run instead of fossil fuels to help combat climate change.

Everything from cars, SUVs and small trucks, bicycles, motorcycle, scooters, boats, hoverboards (or self-balancing electric boards), trains, campers and RVs, can be run on electricity today! Companies are even working on creating electric semi-trucks (to transport goods) and small electric airplanes that someday soon could be used to fly shorter distances.

ELECTRICITY

- Create innovative lighting systems for airport runways that are visible in all weather conditions.

- Experiment and develop new kinds of batteries such as the aluminum-ion batteries that researchers in Sweden are working on. This type of battery would be safer, use materials that are readily available, and, ideally, have twice the energy density of lithium-ion batteries.

- Engineer wireless communications systems that allow internet access from anywhere on your smart phone or tablet.

- Develop renewable energy systems from solar, wind, or wave power for remote places such as islands or satellites in space.

The oldest operating wind turbine, known as the Tvindkraft, is in Jutland, Denmark. It's been generating power for more than 40 years.

- Explore space like electrical engineer Judith Resnik, who was one of the first female astronauts. She conducted scientific experiments and operated the exterior mechanical arm, which she helped design.

Electricity is an important part of our everyday lives. We use it to power many things. It's even inside our own bodies!

We already know a lot about it, but there's still so much to discover. Improving ways to generate and transfer electricity, and finding ways to make it safer to use for us and our planet—these are just a few of things scientists are working on today. But what about tomorrow?

Now that you've learned about electricity, maybe you'll help lead us into the future!

ESSENTIAL QUESTION

How can we generate electricity in more Earth-friendly ways?

TEXT TO WORLD

How do you think we'll power our homes and businesses in the future?

92

SOLAR OVEN

This oven won't bake a cake, but it's perfect for making s'mores. And it's a more energy-efficient way of making them than over a campfire because it doesn't require any wood and doesn't produce pollution.

❯ **Paint the outside of your box and the lid black.** Let them dry.

❯ **Making sure the shiny side is facing up, line the inside of the box and the inside of the lid with aluminum foil.** Try to keep the foil smooth and tape it to the edges.

❯ **Cut a flap in the box lid.** The flap should be about 1 inch in from three edges of the lid. Fold the flap up and tape the loose foil to the flap.

❯ **Put the lid on the box.** Push the flap up and use the popsicle stick to prop it open.

❯ **Place your solar oven in a sunny, warm place outside.** It will work best on a hot day. Position it so the flap reflects the sun into the box.

❯ **Carefully place a graham cracker inside the box.** Lay the chocolate and marshmallows on top of the graham cracker.

❯ **Tape a piece of plastic wrap across the opening of the box.** This will help keep bugs out of the oven and off your food. It will also help trap heat so your oven works better.

❯ **Wait and watch.** It might take a little while for the chocolate to melt. It depends on the temperature that day and how sunny it is. Eat up and enjoy!

TOOL KIT
- paintbrush
- black paint
- shoebox with a lid
- aluminum foil
- masking tape
- scissors
- popsicle stick
- graham crackers, chocolate, marshmallows
- plastic wrap

People have experimented with solar heat traps and solar ovens for hundreds of years.

Try This!

Here are two more recipes you can try in your solar oven.

English Muffin Pizza: Pull apart an English muffin into two halves. Spread pizza sauce on each half. Add cheese. Place your pizzas on a napkin, paper plate, or piece of foil inside your solar oven until the cheese is melted.

Nachos: Spread out a handful of tortilla chips on a paper plate, napkin, or piece of foil. Sprinkle with shredded cheese and salsa. Place it inside your solar oven until the cheese melts. Add sour cream.

MAKE AN
ANEMOMETER

An anemometer is a device that shows how fast the wind is blowing. You can make your own anemometer and chart wind speed at your house.

❯ **Roll the modeling clay into a mound about the size of a golf ball.** Attach it to the block of wood. Push the pencil into the center of the clay with the eraser side up.

❯ **Glue or staple the pieces of cardboard together.** You want them to make an X.

❯ **With the cups placed sideways and all facing the same way, staple each cup to the top of each end of the cardboard strips.** Why do you think the cups should face the same way? Use the marker to color one of the cups red. Why do you think just one cup needs to be marked?

❯ **Push the pin through the middle of the cardboard X and into the pencil eraser.** Gently blow on the cups to make sure they spin.

❯ **Take your stopwatch, science journal, and anemometer outside.** Set the anemometer in an open space where it can catch the wind.

❯ **Use the stopwatch to time 1 minute.** Watch the red cup and count how many times it completes a turn in that minute. Write down the number in your science journal.

TOOL KIT

- ° modeling clay
- ° block of wood (just about any size will work)
- ° pencil with an eraser
- ° 2 pieces of thin cardboard, 12 inches by 1½ inches
- ° 4 small paper cups
- ° red marker
- ° flat or ball-head pin
- ° timer

Try This!

Does the time of day affect wind speed? Are some months windier than others? Test the wind speed and keep track.

Start a scientific method worksheet and make a prediction. Then experiment. Copy the chart below into your journal and record your data.

Time of Day or Month	Wind Speed

ELECTRICITY
GLOSSARY QUIZ

Here's something fun you can do with all the words you've learned in this book!

❯ **1 Use the glossary to answer these questions.**

* A device that produces an electric current using chemicals is called a
  _____.

* Electricity travels along a _____.

* An electric current where electricity flows in one direction is called a
  _____ (or DC). An electric current where electricity flows back
  and forth is called a _____ (or AC).

* The object that uses the electricity in a circuit is called the
  _____.

* _____ is the force that moves electrons in an electric current.

* A _____ is someone who studies energy and matter.

* The force caused by the motion of electrons that either attract objects to it or repels
  them is called _____.

* We depend on the _____, a system of power plants and
  circuits, to deliver electricity to our homes and businesses.

* Renewable energy sources such as wind, water, and solar are good for Earth because
  they have little _____.

* A _____ is a machine
  that turns mechanical force (or motion) into
  electricity.

* The form of natural energy caused by
  the movement of tiny particles is called
  _____. (Hint: It
  provides power for lights, appliances, video
  games, and many other electric devices!)

* Magnets that can be turned on or
  off by using electricity are called
  _____.

Try This!

Create a crossword puzzle based
on words you learned in this
book for your family or friends.

95

WIND TURBINE

Wind turbines are a type of generator. Here's a fun way to make a wind turbine that can generate enough electricity to light up a small bulb.

> **Cut your card stock into a 6-by-6-inch square.** Use a ruler and pencil to draw a line that goes from the top left corner to the bottom right corner. Make another line that goes from the bottom left corner to the top right corner. You should now have an X.

> **Cut each line until it is 1 inch from the center of the X.** You'll have four flaps when you're done.

> **Fold one corner of each flap over until it touches the center of the X.** Use a bit of glue to help keep them in place while you fold. The points should all overlap a little at the center. Carefully push the nail through the flap ends. Use tape to secure the blades to the nail.

> **Push the nail through the cardboard roll, about 1½ inches from the top.** The nail should go straight across and poke out the other side of the roll. Leave a little space between the head of the nail and the roll. Blow on your blades to make sure the nail can turn freely. If it can't, use the scissors to make the holes bigger or pull the blades away from the roll a bit.

> **Inside the roll, attach a magnet to each side of the nail.** Use tape to keep them in place if you need to. Blow on your blades again to make sure the nail with the magnets can still turn freely.

> **Leave the first 6 inches of wire free.** Tape the wire down. Then, starting at the top, wrap the rest of the magnetic wire around the roll up to the top 3 inches of the roll. Go around the nail hole, too, but make sure the nail can still spin freely. The wire should go around the roll multiple times. Secure the end with a piece of tape, leaving a 3-inch piece of loose wire at the end.

TOOL KIT

- card stock
- flat-head nail, 1 inch longer than the diameter of cardboard roll
- sturdy, cardboard roll, 12-inches long
- 2 magnets that can fit inside the cardboard roll
- magnetic copper wire
- metal nail file
- 10-mm LED bulb (3 volt)
- electric tape
- fan or hair dryer

❱ **Use the metal nail file to gently scrap the bottom inch of the loose pieces of wire.** This will remove the thin layer of clear coating that's on the wire.

❱ **Tape one end of the wire to the positive lead of the LED.** Tape the other piece of wire to the negative lead of the LED.

❱ **Set your wind turbine in front of a fan or hair dryer.** Turn on the fan or hair dryer so the blades of your wind turbine turn. What happens to the LED light? It should begin to glow! If it doesn't, try adding more magnetic wire or using bigger magnets. Also check to make sure the LED wires haven't come loose.

Try This!

Does the speed of the "wind" affect the brightness of the LED? Try blowing the blades with your breath or at a lower speed with the fan or hair dryer and see what happens.

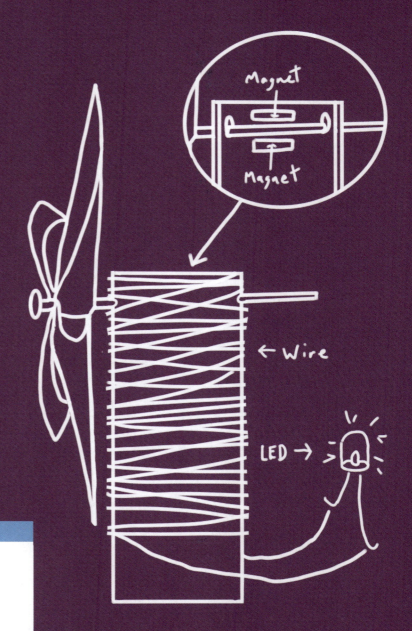

97

GLOSSARY

advantage: something helpful.

alternating current (AC): an electric current where electricity flows back and forth.

amber: a piece of fossilized tree sap or resin.

amperes (amps): the measurement of the amount of electric current.

anode: the end of a battery marked with a minus sign.

appliance: an electric device such as a toaster, microwave, or washing machine.

armature: the spinning part of a motor, made of tightly coiled wires.

arc: a curved path, sometimes made by electricity jumping from one thing to another.

atmosphere: a layer of gas surrounding Earth.

atom: a small particle of matter. Atoms are the extremely tiny building blocks of everything.

attract: to pull together.

axle: a rod on which something spins.

battery: a device that stores and produces electricity using chemicals.

BCE: put after a date, BCE stands for Before Common Era and counts down to zero. CE stands for Common Era and counts up from zero. This book was printed in 2022 CE.

blackout: a loss of electric power.

breaker panel: the electric box that distributes the electricity coming into a house or other building to each outlet and switch.

brush: a soft, springy, metal wire that, with a commutator, acts as a switch inside a motor.

calibrate: to fix an instrument to a standard reading.

capacitor: a device that stores electric energy until it's needed.

carbon dioxide: a gas formed by the burning of fossil fuels, the rotting of plants and animals, and the breathing out of animals or humans.

cathode: the end of a battery marked with a plus sign.

cell: in a battery, a single unit of a battery made up of an anode and a cathode that are separated by an electrolyte.

chemical reaction: the rearrangement of atoms in a substance to make a new chemical substance.

circa: around that year. Abbreviated with a "c."

circuit: a loop that starts and finishes at the same place.

climate change: the long-term change in the earth's weather patterns.

collaboration: working with others.

commutator: the part of a motor that reverses the electric current.

compact fluorescent light (CFL): a light bulb that uses less electricity and lasts longer than an incandescent light bulb.

compass: an instrument that uses a magnetized needle to find north.

conductor: something that electricity moves through easily, such as copper wire.

current: the steady flow of water in one direction or the flow of electricity.

diameter: the straight line that goes from one side of a circle, through its center, to the other side.

diode: a semiconductor device that allows the flow of current in one direction.

direct current (DC): an electric current where electricity flows in one direction.

disadvantage: something that causes difficulty or trouble.

disc: a round, thin piece of material.

discharge: the removal of electrons from an object.

dissect: to cut something apart to study what is inside.

drought: a period of time when no precipitation falls on a region, causing problems for farms and wildlife.

GLOSSARY

dynamic electricity: the movement of an electric charge through a conductor.

efficient: wasting as little as possible.

electrical engineer: an engineer who designs systems and processes that use electricity.

electric charge: an amount of stored electricity caused by an imbalance of electrons, either too many or not enough. The electrons flow to fix the imbalance.

electric current: the flow of an electric charge through a conductor.

electric circuit: the pathway electricity follows.

electrician: a person who installs, fixes, or maintains electric wiring systems.

electricity: a form of energy caused by the movement of tiny particles. It provides power for lights, appliances, video games, and many other electric devices.

electrocution: to be injured or killed by electricity.

electrode: a conductor through which electricity enters and leaves an object such as a battery.

electrolyte: a liquid or paste in a battery that allows for the flow of electric current.

electromagnet: a type of magnet where the magnetic field is produced by electricity.

electromagnetism: magnetism created by an electric current.

electron: a negatively charged particle in an atom, part of a shell moving around the center of an atom.

electronic: describes a device that uses computer parts to control the flow of electricity.

electroscope: a device that is able to detect electric charges.

electrostatics: the study of electric charges that are not moving.

element: a pure substance that is made of atoms that are all the same.

energy: the ability to do things, to work.

engineer: a person who uses science, math, and creativity to design and build things.

engineering: the use of science, math, and creativity in the design and construction of things.

environmental impact: effect on the environment.

expand: to spread out and take up more space.

filament: the wire used as the conducting material inside a light bulb.

force: a push or a pull.

fossil fuel: a source of energy that comes from the fossils of plants and animals that lived millions of years ago. These include coal, oil, and natural gas.

galvanized: coated with zinc.

generate: to create something.

generator: a device that turns motion into electricity.

geothermal energy: energy from below the surface of the earth. It can heat and cool by using differences in temperature between a structure and the earth.

greenhouse gas: a gas in the atmosphere that traps heat and contributes to warming temperatures.

grounded: a circuit in which the current flows directly into the ground.

halogen bulb: a gas-filled incandescent bulb.

horizontal: straight from side to side.

horsepower: a unit of power equal to 746 watts.

hot springs: water under the earth's surface that's heated by underground volcanic activity.

humid: having a high level of moisture in the air.

hydrogen: the most common element in the universe, and one of the elements of water.

hydropower: energy produced by the movement of water.

implement: to put into effect.

incandescent: a source of electric light that works by heating a filament.

99

GLOSSARY

innovation: a new invention or way of doing something.

insulator: a material that prevents heat, sound, or electricity from passing through it easily.

interact: when things that are together affect each other.

ion: an atom that has either fewer electrons than protons or more electrons than protons, and thus has a positive or negative electric charge.

landfill: a place where trash and other waste materials are buried and covered with soil.

light-emitting diode (LED): a bulb that provides very efficient lighting.

lightning: an electric charge from a cloud.

lightning rod: a rod or pole used to move the electric charge from lightning safely into the ground.

load: the object that uses the electricity in a circuit.

magnet: any material that attracts metal.

magnetic field: the invisible area around a magnet that pulls objects to it or pushes them away.

magnetic levitation: the use of magnetic fields generated by superconducting magnets to cause an object (such as a vehicle) to float above a solid surface.

magnetic north: the direction the north end of a compass will point in response to Earth's magnetic field.

magnetic resonance imaging (MRI) machine: a machine used to see inside the body.

magnetism: a force caused by the motion of electrons that either attracts objects or repels them.

matter: anything that has weight and takes up space.

mechanical: related to machines or tools.

mechanical energy: energy that uses physical parts you can see, such as the parts of a machine. It is related to motion and height.

medieval: the period of time in European history from about 350 CE to about 1450 CE. Also called the Middle Ages.

molecule: a group of atoms bound together. Molecules combine to form matter.

momentum: a force that keeps an object moving after it has begun to move.

motor: a machine that turns electric energy into motion.

nanobot: a tiny robot, too small to see without a microscope.

nanomotor: a microscopic motor.

natural resource: a material such as coal, timber, water, or land that is found in nature and is useful to humans.

nerve: a fiber that transmits messages from the brain to the body and vice versa.

neurologist: a doctor who studies and cares for the human nervous system.

neutral: not having a positive or negative charge.

neutron: a particle inside the nucleus of an atom that has no charge.

nonrenewable: a resource such as coal that, once used, is gone forever.

nuclear: energy produced when the nucleus of an atom is split apart.

nucleus: the center of an atom, made up of protons and neutrons. The plural is nuclei.

organic: something that is or was living, such as wood, grass, or insects.

outlet: a device in a wall that an electric cord plugs into.

oxygen: a colorless gas found in the air, needed by animals and humans to breathe.

parallel circuit: a circuit with a pathway to the power source for each load.

particle: a tiny piece of matter.

100

GLOSSARY

physicist: a scientist who studies how matter and energy behave within the universe.

pollution: harmful materials that damage the air, water, and soil. These include chemicals and factory waste.

potential energy: the amount of energy that is possible.

power: electricity made available to use.

power grid: a system of power plants and circuits.

power plant: a place where electric power is produced to be spread out and used.

pressure: a force that pushes on an object.

proton: a positively charged particle in the nucleus of an atom.

radioactive: a substance made of atoms that gives off nuclear energy.

radio wave: a type of invisible wave used to transmit radio and television signals. Radio waves are also used for navigation.

reactor core: part of the system that splits atoms to generate energy.

rectifier: a device that converts AC electricity into DC.

renewable: something that isn't used up, that can be replaced.

repel: to force away or apart.

resistance: a force that slows down another force.

semiconductor: a material that conducts some electricity.

series circuit: a circuit with a single path from the power source to the load and back to the power source.

shell: the area around a nucleus through which electrons move.

short circuit: a direct connection between two points in a circuit that aren't supposed to be directly connected.

solar: relating to the sun.

solar array: a collection of solar panels.

solar cell: a device that converts the energy of the sun into electric energy.

solar power: energy that comes from the sun.

static electricity: the buildup of an electric charge on the surface of an object.

substation: a special power plant where electricity is reduced in voltage so it can be used in homes, offices, and so on.

superconductor: a material that can carry electricity without resistance.

switch: a control that opens or closes a circuit.

technology: the tools, methods, and systems used to solve a problem or do work.

Tesla coil: a device used for research that can produce high-voltage electricity.

theory: an idea that could explain how or why something happens.

transformer: a device that changes the voltage of an alternating current.

transistor: a device that controls the flow of electricity.

turbine: a device that uses pressure on blades to spin generators and create electricity.

ultrasonic: describes a sound too high for humans to hear.

ultraviolet light: a kind of light with short wavelengths. It can't be seen with the naked eye.

vertical: straight up and down.

voltage: the force, measured in volts, that moves electrons in an electric current.

wattage: the amount of power, measured in watts, that's created or used.

wave: a curving movement in water, air, ground, or other object.

winding: wire wrapped around an armature.

zinc: a chemical element that helps protect iron and steel from damage.

GLOSSARY

Metric Conversions

Use this chart to find the metric equivalents to the English measurements in this book.
If you need to know a half measurement, divide by two.
If you need to know twice the measurement, multiply by two.
How do you find a quarter measurement? How do you find three times the measurement?

English	Metric
1 inch	2.5 centimeters
1 foot	30.5 centimeters
1 yard	0.9 meter
1 mile	1.6 kilometers
1 pound	0.5 kilogram
1 teaspoon	5 milliliters
1 tablespoon	15 milliliters
1 cup	237 milliliters

BOOKS

Butterworth, Chris. *How Does My Home Work?* Candlewick Press, 2017.

Cole, Joanna. *The Magic School Bus and the Electric Field Trip*. Scholastic Inc., 1997.

Dahl, Oyvind Nydal. *Electronics for Kids: Play with Simple Circuits and Experiments with Electricity!* No Starch Press, 2016.

Drummond, Allan. *Energy Island: How One Community Harnessed the Wind and Changed Their World*. Square Fish Books, 2015.

Graham, Ian. *You Wouldn't Want to Live Without Electricity*. Franklin Watts, 2014.

Hawbaker, Emily. *Energy Lab for Kids: 40 Exciting Experiments to Explore, Create, Harness, and Unleash Energy*. Quarry Books, 2017.

O'Quinn, Amy M. *Nikola Tesla for Kids: His Life, Ideas, and Inventions.* Chicago Review Press, 2019.

RESOURCES

WEBSITES

DK findout! Electricity
dkfindout.com/us/science/electricity

U.S. Energy Information Administration: Electricity Explained
eia.gov/energyexplained/electricity

NASA: Electrical Power to Orbiter Systems
mars.nasa.gov/mro/mission/spacecraft/parts/electricalpower

Electricity/Science Trek
wosu.pbslearningmedia.org/resource/idptv11.sci.phys.energy.d4kele/electricity

Ducksters: Electricity for Kids Intro
ducksters.com/science/electricity_101.php

Ducksters: Electricity in Nature
ducksters.com/science/physics/electricity_in_nature.php

Technology for Kids: The Power of Circuits
youtube.com/watch?v = HOFp8bHTN30

DK Find Out: Electricity
dkfindout.com/us/science/electricity

NASA Climate Kids
climatekids.nasa.gov/power-savers

Practical Engineering: How Electricity Generation Really Works
youtube.com/watch?v = AHFZVn38dTM

MUSEUMS

The Franklin Institute Science Museum, Philadelphia, PA: fi.edu

National Museum of American History and (Smithsonian),
Washington, D.C.: americanhistory.si.edu

American Museum of Science and Energy, Oak Ridge, TN: amse.org

SPARK Museum of Electrical Invention, Bellingham, WA: sparkmuseum.org

National Electronics Museum, Baltimore, MD: nationalelectronicsmuseum.org

RESOURCES

ESSENTIAL QUESTIONS

Introduction: What are some ways electricity is important to our daily lives?

Chapter 1: What are some ways we can see or experience static electricity?

Chapter 2: How is the electricity we use to power things such as appliances different from static electricity?

Chapter 3: How does electricity travel across the country and into our homes and businesses?

Chapter 4: How is electromagnetism related to electricity?

Chapter 5: How do motors and generators use magnets?

Chapter 6: How can we generate electricity in more Earth-friendly ways?

QR CODE GLOSSARY

Page 3: youtube.com/watch?v=FS-tmBD9Cjk#action=share

Page 11: scienceworld.ca/resource/static-electricity

Page 12: youtube.com/watch?v=y20lKZB5BR0

Page 15: founders.archives.gov/documents/Franklin/01-04-02-0135

Page 20: youtube.com/watch?v=PaFeNFVbZOs

Page 21: bbc.co.uk/programmes/p00ksnyn

Page 30: bbc.com/news/av/world-australia-45648303/world-s-biggest-battery-a-look-around-tesla-project

Page 45: youtube.com/watch?v=waSmFAPWqDE

Page 46: cennentialbulb.org

Page 48: youtube.com/watch?v=YB9tnteKaWo

Page 57: nationalgeographic.org/activity/magnetic-fields-lab/?utm_source=BibblioRCM_Row

Page 60: youtube.com/watch?v=cxELqN7wjS0

Page 62: youtube.com/watch?v=XjwF-STGtfE

Page 71: youtube.com/watch?v=5F7XwjUgK8o

Page 74: youtube.com/watch?v=ty1Fk0JZfQk

Page 75: youtube.com/watch?v=CWulQ1ZSE3c

Page 84: youtube.com/watch?v=5CzuwztCw-E

Page 86: nationalgeographic.org/video/edu-wind-turbines

Page 91: mapmakerclassic.nationalgeographic.org

INDEX

A

activities
Boogie Balls Box, 21
Create Your Own Science Journal, 7
Electricity Glossary Quiz, 95
Electromagnet, 65
Electrophorus, 80
Flashlight, 52–53
Magnetic Field Viewer, 63
Magnetic Slime, 66
Make a Compass, 64
Make an Anemometer, 94
Make an Electroscope, 22–23
Make a Vinegar Battery, 36–37
Make a Voltaic Pile, 34–35
Paper Clip Switch, 54
Simple Closed Circuit, 51
Simple Motor, 78–79
Solar Oven, 93
Static Electricity in Action, 24
Switch It Up Experiment, 8
Water Turbine, 76–77
Watts in Action, 38
Wind Turbine, 96–97
alternating current (AC), iv, 46–48, 49, 69, 73
amperage/amps, 29–30
animals, iv, 3, 26–27, 31–32, 87. *See also* human body

B

batteries, iv–v, 2, 28–37, 40, 46, 84–85, 91–92
biomass power, 87, 89–90
blackouts, 4

C

capacitors, 14, 72, 75, 80
careers, v, 2, 5, 28, 50, 60, 76, 91–92
Centennial Light Bulb, 46

circuits, 39–54
AC or DC, 46–48, 49
definition of, 4, 40
light bulbs and, 42–45, 52–53
open vs. closed, 40–41, 51
parallel, 41–42
parts of, 41
power delivery and, 43, 47, 48–50
series, 40–41, 42
short, 43
switches and, 40–42, 54. *See also* switches
climate change, 82, 90, 91
compasses, 56, 61–62, 64
compass roses, 64
conductors, 4, 20, 26–28, 29, 32, 45
currents, 25–38
alternating vs. direct, iv, 46–48, 49, 69, 73
batteries and, 31–37. *See also* batteries
conductors, insulators, and, 26–28, 29, 32. *See also* conductors; insulators
definition of, 25–26
volts, amps, and watts of, 28–30, 38

D

Davy, Humphry, 58
direct current (DC), 46–48, 69, 73
dynamic electricity, 24. *See also* currents

E

Earth-friendly electricity, 81–97
biomass power for, 87, 89–90
careers related to, 91–92
climate change and, 82, 90, 91
geothermal power for, 88–89

hydropower for, 85, 86, 92. *See also* hydropower/water turbines
light bulbs and, 44–45
nuclear power for, 90. *See also* nuclear power
renewable vs. nonrenewable resources and, 81–82
solar power for, 83–85, 88, 92, 93. *See also* solar power
wind power for, 86–87, 92, 94, 96–97. *See also* wind power/wind turbines
Edison, Thomas, iv, 1, 42–43, 47, 73
electricity
circuits of. *See* circuits
definition of, 1, 9
dynamic, 24. *See also* currents
Earth-friendly. *See* Earth-friendly electricity
electromagnetism and. *See* electromagnetism
jobs or careers with, v, 2, 5, 28, 50, 60, 76, 91–92
motors, generators, and. *See* motors and generators
power from. *See* power/power plants/power grid
safety issues with. *See* electric shocks; safety issues
static. *See* static electricity
timeline of, iv–v
electric shocks, 2–3, 12, 19, 29, 32. *See also* electrocution
electric vehicles, v, 30, 33, 60, 91
electrocution, 26–27, 29
electromagnetism, 55–66
compasses and, 56, 61–62, 64
definition of, 4, 59
discovery of, iv, 56, 58–59
electromagnets or super magnets, 59–60, 65
magnetic fields and, 57–59, 61–62, 63
motors, generators, and, 58, 60, 67–71, 75
North and South Poles and, 61–62

105

INDEX

electrons, 9–12
energy, 1. *See also* electricity; mechanical energy; potential energy

F
Faraday, Michael, iv, 58–59
Franklin, Benjamin, iv, 1, 14–16, 20

G
Galvani, Luigi, iv, 31–32
generators. *See* motors and generators
geothermal power, 88–89
Gilbert, William, iv, 13, 22
Gray, Stephen, 21

H
Holmes, John Henry, 8
horsepower, 74
human body, 3, 4, 5, 26–27, 63, 75, 91, 92
hybrid vehicles, 33, 60
hydropower/water turbines, v, 71–72, 76–77, 85, 86, 92

I
insulators, 4, 15, 26–28
International Space Station, 84

J
jobs, v, 2, 5, 28, 50, 60, 76, 91–92

L
Leyden jars, iv, 13–14
lightning, iv, 1, 3, 14–18, 20
lights/light switches/light bulbs, iv–v, 8, 40–45, 46, 52–54

M
maglev (magnetic levitation) trains, 62
magnetism. *See* electromagnetism
Maxwell, James Clerk, iv, 59
mechanical energy, 70
motors and generators, 67–80
    capacitors and, 72, 75, 80
    definitions of, 4
    electromagnetism and, 58, 60, 67–71, 75
    generators, 4, 12, 71–72, 76–77, 96–97
    horsepower of, 74
    inventions with, 73–75
    motors, iv–v, 4, 68–71, 74–75, 78–79
    nanobots and, v, 75

N
nanobots/nanomotors, v, 75
North Pole, 61–62
nuclear power, v, 90

O
Oersted, Hans Christian, iv, 56, 58–59

P
parallel circuits, 41–42
Pliny the Elder, 2
potential energy, 28–29
power/power plants/power grid, 3–4, 8, 43, 47, 48–50. *See also* currents; Earth-friendly electricity

R
roller coasters, 61

S
safety issues, 5, 18, 26–29, 49–50, 63, 90. *See also* electric shocks

semiconductors, 45
series circuits, 40–41, 42
short circuits, 43
solar power, iv–v, 45, 83–85, 88, 92, 93
South Pole, 61–62
space, power in, 84, 90, 92
static electricity, 9–24
    definition of, 2
    electric shocks from, 12, 19
    electrons and, 9–12
    experiments with, iv, 13–16, 21–24
    lightning and, 16–18, 20. *See also* lightning
STEM/STEAM, 2
superconductors, 29
switches, 8, 40–42, 54

T
TerraPower, 90
Tesla, Inc., 30, 73
Tesla, Nikola, iv, 47, 73–74
Tesla coils, 73–74
Thales of Miletus, iv, 2, 7
turbines, v, 71–72, 76–77, 85–90, 92, 96–97

V
Van de Graaff generators, 12
Volta, Alessandro, iv, 32, 34, 80
voltage/volts, 28–30

W
water
    as conductor, 26, 28, 32
    molecule of, 10
    power/turbines, v, 71–72, 76–77, 85, 86, 92
    static electricity and, 12, 24
Watt, James, 74
wattage/watts, 30, 38
wave power, 86, 92
Wilcox, Margaret A., 70
Wimshurst, James/Wimshurst machine, iv, 13
wind power/wind turbines, v, 71–72, 86–87, 92, 94, 96–97